D0471874

JONI SEAGER is a Canadian feminist geographer and a university lecturer in Geography, Women's Studies and International Development. She is co-director of the Association of American Geographers' Specialist Group on Women and is Coordinator of Women's Studies at MIT.

ANN OLSON is an American geographer and cart-ographer and a feminist. She has worked for the United States Geological Survey on the US National Atlas and for the United Nations University on the Mountain Hazards Mapping Project.

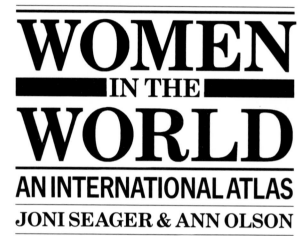

# WOMEN
## IN THE
# WORLD
## AN INTERNATIONAL ATLAS

### JONI SEAGER & ANN OLSON

A PLUTO PRESS PROJECT

Edited by Michael Kidron

**A TOUCHSTONE BOOK**
PUBLISHED BY SIMON & SCHUSTER, INC. NEW YORK

Text copyright © 1986 by Joni Seager and Ann Olson
Maps and graphics copyright © 1986 by Pluto Press Limited

All rights reserved
including the right of reproduction
in whole or in part or in any form

Simon and Schuster/Touchstone Books,
Published by Simon & Schuster, Inc.
Simon & Schuster Building,
Rockefeller Center,
1230 Avenue of the Americas
New York, New York 10020

SIMON AND SCHUSTER, TOUCHSTONE and colophons are registered trademarks of Simon & Schuster, Inc.

Designed by Tilly Northedge of Grundy & Northedge, London
Artwork by Swanston Graphics, Derby
Cover illustration by Stuart Bodek
Coordinated by Anne Benewick

Color origination by Imago Publishing Ltd
Printed and bound in Hong Kong by Mandarin Offset International (HK) Ltd

1 2 3 4 5 6 7 8 9 10 (hardback)
1 2 3 4 5 6 7 8 9 10 (paperback)

Library of Congress Cataloging in Publication Data

Seager, Joni

Women in the world.

1. Women – Social conditions. 2. Women – Economic conditions. 3. Women.
I. Olson, Ann. II. Title. HQ1154.03965 1986 305.4'2 86-6739

ISBN 0-671-60297-7 (hardback)
      0-671-63070-9 (paperback)

# CONTENTS

# CONTENTS

Most women in the world, like most men, lead humble lives. Their daily preoccupations are with economic survival and success, raising healthy and happy children, making sure that personal and family needs are met, and garnering some measure of emotional satisfaction from life. What is striking, though, is how different women's ordinary lives are from men's ordinary lives. And to see women's lives we cannot simply look at the world of men and proceed to women as an afterthought.

This atlas rests on the assumption that we cannot understand our world without understanding the everyday experience of women. Women's contributions are at least as important as those of men: 'They are the providers of food, fuel, water, and often the whole family income – the sustainers and developers of their families, communities, and countries . . . the fate of women is a critical determinant of the fate of whole societies.' (Margaret Snyder, UN Voluntary Fund for Women)

In this atlas, we ask not only *what* is happening between women and men (and between women themselves), but *where* it is happening. Geography matters, we believe. By mapping the world of women, patterns are revealed that are usually obscured in statistical tables or in narratives. The similarities and differences, the continuities and contrasts among women around the world are best shown by – literally – mapping out their lives. Although maps suggest objectivity, no atlas is free from a point of view; our feminism legitimately informs our work. We do not presume a global community of women. What we do see, however, is that everywhere women are worse off than men: women have less power, less autonomy, more work, less money, and more responsibility. Women everywhere have a smaller share of the pie; if the pie is very small (as in poor countries), women's share is smaller still. Women in rich countries have a higher standard of living than do women in poor countries, but nowhere are women equal to men.

There are other commonalities, formed from common experiences. Women everywhere share primary responsibility for having and rearing children, for forming and maintaining families, for contraception. They share, too, the lead in fighting for women's rights, for other civil rights, and for peace. Rich and poor, they also suffer rape, health traumas from illegal abortions, the degradation of pornography.

Nevertheless, global generalizations are not meant to obscure the very real differences that exist between women, country by country, region by region. For example:

● In Afghanistan four per cent of eligible girls are enrolled in secondary school; in Australia 88 per cent are;

● In Angola fewer than one per cent of adult women have access to contraceptives; in Belgium 76 per cent do;

7

- Women in Ghana bear an average of over six children; women in West Germany, fewer than two;
- In Jamaica the maternal mortality rate stands at 106 mothers' deaths for every 100,000 births; in Norway there are fewer than 8 deaths per 100,000 births.

Inequalities in wealth and access to opportunities should not be minimized. In poor countries (usually described as the 'Third World' or the 'developing' world – labels we have tried to avoid), most people are in a situation of dependency, powerlessness, vulnerability and inequality of income. All of these conditions of 'underdevelopment' are experienced by women to a greater extent. Yet the distinction between the 'First' and 'Third' worlds is usually made on the basis of economic indicators which often have little to do with women's lives, and that do not necessarily help to assess their situation and status. In fact, looking at the world through women's eyes raises questions about the validity of conventional distinctions between 'developed' and 'underdeveloped' countries:

- In both Saudi Arabia and Austria women make up less than 20 per cent of university teachers, but almost 100 per cent of pre-primary school teachers;
- In Haiti women constitute five per cent of all employees in the media; in Japan two per cent;
- In Peru and Canada, in the UK and Uruguay, women have the same proportion of representation in government;
- The governments in Romania and Chad have similarly repressive population policies, restricting women's access to contraceptives and family planning.

In the world of women there are few 'developed' nations.

But women's lives are not fully captured by bleak statistics. Over the past two decades there have been tremendous advances in education for women. More and more women are being paid to work. Governments are being pressured to recognize and protect women's rights. But most importantly and positively, women are coming out of the shadows and fighting for what is rightfully theirs. It is independent organizing on the part of women that has given us equal opportunity laws, the right to abortion, and battered-women's shelters.

There are few instances where men in authority have shared power with women voluntarily. Women have not automatically gained through national struggles or under 'revolutionary' governments: a rising tide does not necessarily raise all boats, and women have frequently been left behind even when broad social advances have been made. The attitudes of men in power to women seem to be remarkably similar across a wide geographic and political spectrum. Within one month in the autumn of 1985 the newspapers reported the words of a high ranking American official: 'women don't understand the issues at the peace summit ... or what is happening in human rights'; the Greek president exhorting women to have more babies to help bolster military manpower to face a future threat from Turkey; and President Marcos of the Philippines saying that he was 'embarrassed' to be running in a political campaign against a woman.

This world atlas of women not only explores the similarities and differences between and among women – it also raises fundamental questions about who has authority, who has power and who does not, who is on top and who is at the bottom. We have tried to capture the world of women within as broad a reach as possible. Maps in the chapters on *Marriage* and *Motherhood* consider not only the act of marriage, but also some of its consequences – which include domestic violence and early death in childbirth. In *Work*, unpaid work in the household, universally considered to be women's work, is contrasted with the share of paid work done by women. Under *Resources* and *Welfare*, we map health and education, women refugees, and global trends toward the feminization of poverty. We look at *Authority* in the World: in governments, in the militaries, and in the media. Prostitution, rape, and beauty contests are dealt with in *Body Politics*. In the section on *Change*, we have tried to capture the various ways in which women forge social change – on their own behalf and for others.

Each map-spread focuses on a central topic, and usually includes two or three sub-topics supporting the main one. A short text provides a brief introduction and draws attention to the inter-relationships between the graphics. Comments and background information are provided in the notes. We have also tried to include here information that we could not find space for on the maps – so the notes also form a separate resource section.

Throughout the research for this atlas we have been hampered by the inadequacy and inaccessibility of international data on women. *Some* information exists on almost all topics but, with the exception of a few standard indicators, information on women is conspicuously absent from conventional sources. A large share of the data in this book was gleaned from feminist writing in small presses, newsletters from women's organizations the world over, and 'alternative' journals of various descriptions: this makes for interesting reading, but laborious research. For all maps, multiple sources (an average of more than ten per map) were used to cross-check reliability and to fill in uneven information patterns.

The official invisibility of women perpetuates the myth that what women do is less important, less noteworthy, less significant. Women are *made* invisible by policies and priorities that discount the importance of collecting information about them. Although the United Nations Decade for Women (1975–85) resulted in a considerable increase in international information on women, women are still not generally included in the information mainstream. Largely as a result of these data constraints, there are a number of topics that we consider important but could not include. Readers will notice that large areas of interest, such as women and religion, and women and shelter, are missing. We do not offer information about women in sports, or women in the arts. We have nothing to map on lesbians or disabled women. We can do little about these omissions except to note them, and to assure readers that they are not an indication of disregard on our part.

The planning for this atlas took two years, the research another year and a half. Over this time our understanding of the issues that affect women, and of the importance of making international comparisons, has deepened. We have often been struck by the realization that women's lives are complex, and it is never simple to draw comparisons across cultures. As Western, white women, we have struggled with our own limitations in understanding the experiences of women in a very wide and diverse world. Primarily, though, we have been heartened by the examples of women coping, women changing, and women solving their own problems. In the world of women, things are both better and worse than one might think.

There are many people without whom this atlas would not have appeared:

Mike Kidron, our editor, put in long hours and hard work editing the sometimes incomprehensible manuscripts we sent – and he did so with much creativity and in good humour; to him also goes full credit for initiating and overseeing the entire atlas series. Anne Benewick coordinatèd all of the production – a monumental task on a project such as this – and added a voice of reason when the rest of us were becoming unreasonable. Tilly Northedge designed all of the wonderful graphics and displays that make this atlas so exceptional. Nina Kidron provided support, substantial insight, and kept us on the books. Cynthia Enloe and Dan Smith provided the initial introduction to Pluto Press. Angela Quinn provided editorial assistance during the early stages.

Ed Deagle and Alberta Arthurs at the Rockefeller Foundation deserve a lot of credit, and our sincere thanks, for going out of their way to support a somewhat unorthodox proposal; Alison Bernstein shepherded our funding requests through the Ford Foundation. It was the financial support from these two foundations that allowed us to undertake the full-time research for this book.

The Institute for Policy Studies (Washington DC) and the Wellesley College Center for Research on Women (Wellesley, Massachusetts) provided institutional support. Our special thanks to Bob Borosage, Nancy Lewis and Doris Porter at IPS, and to Laura Lein and Jan Putnam at Wellesley.

Our advisory board lent their good names and support to this unlikely venture. Much appreciation to: Elise Boulding; Barbara Ehrenreich; Cynthia Enloe; Rayna Green; Perdita Huston; Mildred Marcy; Joann Vanek.

Christopher Laxton supported the project with his love and assistance, editorial and computing insight, and skilful baby care – and helped in the creation of another wonderful project, Sarah Lindsay. Cynthia Enloe offered constant encouragement, unqualified support . . . and considerable data.

Our most substantial debt is to countless unnamed feminists who, for years, have been the only ones insisting that it is important to ask questions about where the women are. Without the collective support of the women's movement, and the pathbreaking efforts of a persistent few, we would have neither the knowledge nor the confidence to undertake this atlas.

And lastly, but certainly not least, our thanks to each other. It is our friendship and our faith in each other that kept us going through the three years of this project.

Joni Seager
Ann Olson

London, January 1986

# ACKNOWLEDGEMENTS

Many people and organizations in addition to those already acknowledged contributed data, encouragement and advice. Without their help this atlas would be substantially shorter. Our thanks to:

Anne Marie Amantia, Population Crisis Committee, Washington DC; American College of Nurse Midwives, Washington DC; American Home Economics Association, Washington DC; Alice Andrews, George Mason University; Rita Arditti, FINNRAGE (Feminist International Network of Resistance to Reproductive and Genetic Engineering); Arlington County Public Library, Central Library, Reference Staff; Kathleen Barry, International Feminist Network Against Female Sexual Slavery; Jade Blaney, Stratford, Ontario; Philippa Brewster, London; Judith Bruce, Population Council, New York City; Gilda Bruckman, Boston; Ximena Bunster, Santiago; Canadian-American Center, University of Maine; Carol Carp, American Public Health Association, Washington DC; Miriam Chamberlain, National Council for Research on Women, New York City; Antoinette Clancy, Women's Political Party, Ireland; Paul Clarke, Reston, Virginia; Dean Cooke, Toronto; Mona Domosh, Worcester, Massachusetts; Renate Duelli Klein, FINNRAGE; Tracy Enright, Pan American Health Organization, Washington DC; Equity Policy Center, Washington DC; Maria Estroza, Pan American Health Organization, Washington DC; Feminist International Network of Resistance to Reproductive and Genetic Engineering (FINNRAGE); Elena Fletcher, National Cancer Institute, Bethesda, Maryland.

Jill Gay, Institute for Policy Studies, Washington DC; Elizabeth Grant, Delegation of the Commission of the European Communities, New York; Barbara Haber, Schlesinger Library, Radcliffe College; Susan Hanson, Clark University; Sandra Harding, University of Delaware; Jane Hawksley, London; Fran Hosken, Women's International Network, Lexington, Massachusetts; Jaimie Hubbard, Toronto; International Labor Organization, Geneva and Washington DC; International Planned Parenthood Federation, New York City and London; Constant Jacquet, National Council of Churches; Evelina Kane, Women Against Pornography, New York City; Jeanne Kasperson, CENTED, Clark University; Doris Krebs, International Council of Nurses; David Lee, National Clearinghouse on Marital Rape; London Rape Crisis Centre; Helen MacSherry, United Nations Information Center, Washington DC; Mike McDermott, Reston, Virginia; Peggy McIntosh, Wellesley College Center for Research on Women; Minority Rights Group, London; Janice Monk, Southwest Institute for Research on Women, Tucson, Arizona; Moynihan's Bar, Worcester, Massachusetts; Aimee Nestingen, Pan American Health Organization, Washington DC.

Office of Women in Development, Agency for International Development, Washington DC; Jon Olson, Pasadena, California; Mary M. Olson, Washington DC; Peter Olson, Arlington, Virginia; William C. Olson, American University; Phyllis Palmer, Women's Studies Program, George Washington University; Deborah Pearlman, Brandeis University; Population Reference Bureau, Library staff; April Powers, Institute for Policy Studies, Washington DC; Betty Reardon, Teacher's College, Columbia University; Caryn Riley, International Labor Organization, Washington DC; Keven Roth, Herndor, Virginia; Lois Roth, Washington DC; E. Royston, Division of Family Health, World Health Organization; Bob Schaaf, Library of Congress, Washington DC; Joan Seager, Toronto; Julie Seager, Nassau; Ruth Sivard, World Priorities, Washington DC; Barbara Sloan, Delegation of the Commission of the European Communities; Sian Steward, Boston; Wendy Stickel, Agency for International Development; Norma Swenson, Boston Women's Healthbook Collective; United States Geological Survey; Judith Wachs, Boston; Anne Walker, International Women's Tribune Center, New York City; Betsy Warrior, Boston; Lois Wasserspring, Wellesley College; Barbara Wein, World Policy Institute, New York City; Wellesley College, Reference Library staff; Karen White, International Center for Research on Women; Women's Institute for Freedom of the Press, Washington DC; World Health Organization; Laura X, National Clearinghouse on Marital Rape.

# SECOND IN RIGHTS

Constitutional provisions for women's rights and equality, 1985

☐ date of latest provision in any area  　= in general sexual equality  　O in marriage and the family  　↘ in employment

| Country | Date | General | Marriage | Employment |
|---|---|---|---|---|
| **AFRICA** | | | | |
| Algeria | 1976 | = | | |
| Benin | 1979 | | O | |
| Botswana | 1971 | = | | |
| Burkina Faso | 1970 | = | | |
| Burundi | 1981 | = | | |
| Cameroon | 1975 | = | | |
| Cape Verde | 1980 | = | | |
| CAR | 1981 | = | | ↘ |
| Comoros | 1978 | = | | |
| Congo | 1979 | = | | ↘ |
| Djibouti | 1977 | = | | |
| Egypt | 1980 | | | |
| Equatorial Guinea | 1982 | = | O | |
| Gabon | 1982 | | | ↘ |
| Gambia | 1970 | = | | |
| Guinea | 1982 | | | |
| Ivory Coast | 1975 | = | | |
| Kenya | 1979 | = | | |
| Liberia | 1983 | = | | ↘ |
| Madagascar | 1975 | = | | |
| Mauritania | 1978 | | | |
| Mauritius | 1977 | = | | |
| Morocco | 1972 | | | |
| Mozambique | 1975 | = | | |
| Rwanda | 1978 | = | | |
| Sao Tome and Principe | 1975 | = | | |
| Senegal | 1981 | = | | |
| Seychelles | 1979 | | | |
| Sierra Leone | 1978 | = | | |
| Somalia | 1979 | = | | ↘ |
| Sudan | 1973 | = | | ↘ |
| Tanzania | 1977 | = | | |
| Togo | 1979 | = | | |
| Tunisia | 1976 | | | |
| Uganda | 1967 | | | |
| Zaire | 1978 | = | | ↘ |
| Zambia | 1979 | = | | |
| Zimbabwe | 1979 | = | | |
| **AMERICAS** | | | | |
| Antigua and Barbuda | 1981 | = | | |
| Argentina | 1968 | | | |
| Bahamas | 1973 | = | | |
| Barbados | 1966 | = | | |
| Belize | 1981 | = | | |
| Bolivia | 1967 | = | O | |
| Brazil | 1982 | = | | ↘ |
| Canada | 1985 | = | | |
| Chile | 1980 | | | |
| Costa Rica | 1977 | | O | ↘ |
| Cuba | 1976 | = | O | ↘ |
| Dominica | 1978 | = | | |
| Dominican Republic | 1966 | | | |
| Ecuador | 1978 | = | O | |
| El Salvador | 1962 | | O | ↘ |
| Guatemala | 1982 | = | | ↘ |
| Guyana | 1980 | = | | ↘ |
| Haiti | 1964 | | O | |
| Honduras | 1982 | = | O | ↘ |
| Jamaica | 1962 | = | | |
| Mexico | 1981 | = | | ↘ |
| Nicaragua | 1979 | = | O | ↘ |
| Panama | 1979 | = | O | ↘ |
| Paraguay | 1977 | | | |
| Peru | 1979 | = | | ↘ |
| St Kitts-Nevis | 1983 | = | | |
| St Lucia | 1978 | = | | |
| St Vincent | 1979 | = | | |
| Surinam | 1982 | = | O | ↘ |
| USA | 1967 | | | |
| Uruguay | 1966 | | | |
| Venezuela | 1961 | = | | ↘ |
| **ASIA AND OCEANIA** | | | | |
| Afghanistan | 1978 | = | | |
| Bahrain | 1973 | | | |
| Burma | 1981 | = | O | |
| China | 1982 | = | O | ↘ |
| Fiji | 1970 | = | | |
| India | 1979 | = | | |
| Indonesia | 1945 | | | |
| Iraq | 1970 | = | | |
| Israel | 1951 | | O | |
| Japan | 1947 | = | O | |
| Jordan | 1952 | | | |
| Kiribati | 1979 | = | | |
| Korea, North | 1972 | = | | |
| Korea, South | 1980 | = | O | |
| Lebanon | 1947 | | | |
| Malaysia | 1981 | | | |
| Maldives | 1975 | | | |
| Mongolia | 1980 | = | | ↘ |
| Nauru | 1968 | = | | |
| Nepal | 1978 | = | | |
| New Zealand | 1977 | | | ↘ |
| Pakistan | 1981 | = | | |
| Papua New Guinea | 1978 | = | | |
| Qatar | 1972 | = | | |
| Singapore | 1980 | | | |
| Solomon Islands | 1978 | = | | |
| Sri Lanka | 1978 | = | | |
| Syria | 1973 | | | ↘ |
| Taiwan | 1947 | = | | |
| Thailand | 1978 | | | |
| Tonga | 1981 | | | |
| Tuvalu | 1978 | = | | |
| United Arab Emirates | 1971 | | | |
| USSR | 1977 | = | O | ↘ |
| Vanuatu | 1979 | = | | |
| Vietnam | 1980 | | O | ↘ |
| Western Samoa | 1981 | = | | |
| Yemen, North | 1970 | = | | |
| Yemen, South | 1970 | | | |
| **EUROPE** | | | | |
| Albania | 1976 | = | O | ↘ |
| Austria | 1974 | = | | |
| Belgium | 1971 | | | |
| Bulgaria | 1971 | = | O | |
| Cyprus | 1960 | = | | |
| Czechoslovakia | 1960 | = | O | ↘ |
| Finland | 1981 | | | |
| France | 1963 | | | |
| Germany, East | 1974 | = | O | ↘ |
| Germany, West | 1973 | = | | |
| Greece | 1975 | = | | ↘ |
| Hungary | 1972 | = | | ↘ |
| Ireland | 1979 | | | |
| Italy | 1947 | = | O | ↘ |
| Lichtenstein | 1965 | | | |
| Luxembourg | 1956 | | | |
| Malta | 1974 | = | | ↘ |
| Monaco | 1962 | | | |
| Netherlands | 1983 | = | | |
| Poland | 1976 | = | | ↘ |
| Portugal | 1982 | = | O | ↘ |
| Romania | 1975 | = | | ↘ |
| Spain | 1978 | = | O | ↘ |
| Sweden | 1975 | = | | |
| Switzerland | 1981 | = | | ↘ |
| Turkey | 1982 | = | | |
| Yugoslavia | 1974 | = | | |
| United Kingdom | 1975 | = | O | ↘ |

Copyright © Pluto Press

# WOMEN IN THE WORLD

For women, there are no developed countries. Although some places are clearly better for them to live in than others, it is not always true that the relatively rich countries of the world provide better circumstances for them as women than do poorer countries.

While many countries provide formally for sexual equality in law, very few governments have legislated to protect specific job and marriage rights; and such law as exists is nullified or blunted in its effect by social and administrative practice. Nowhere do women have full equal rights with men.

Yet women are biologically stronger, live longer than men, and naturally outnumber them. Where they do not, it is only because of the effects of war, or because they have been forced to migrate in search of work, or because they have suffered severe and systematic discrimination.

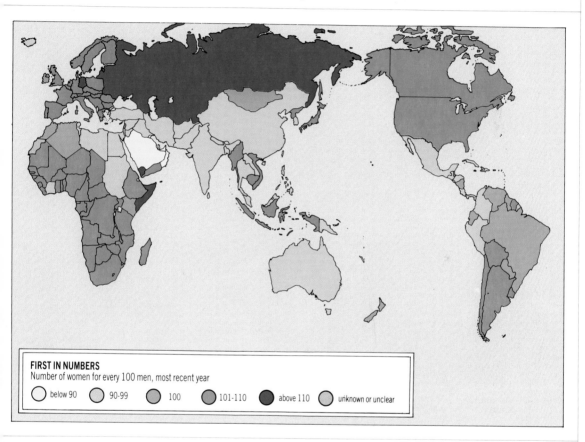

**FIRST IN NUMBERS**
Number of women for every 100 men, most recent year

○ below 90  ○ 90-99  ○ 100  ○ 101-110  ● above 110  ○ unknown or unclear

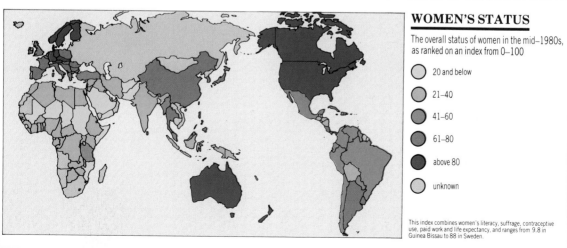

## WOMEN'S STATUS

*The overall status of women in the mid–1980s, as ranked on an index from 0–100*

○ 20 and below

○ 21–40

○ 41–60

○ 61–80

● above 80

○ unknown

This index combines women's literacy, suffrage, contraceptive use, paid work and life expectancy, and ranges from 9.8 in Guinea Bissau to 88 in Sweden.

# EARLY MARRIAGE

Proportion of women, uneducated and educated, who marry young (aged 15-19), selected examples, late 1970s *percentages*

● no schooling ● more than 7 years spent at school

- Bangladesh 75 46
- Colombia 38 9
- Dominican Republic 43 17
- Guyana 100 30
- Jordan 40 12
- Malaysia 20 4
- Mexico 54 8
- Pakistan 49 6
- Panama 39 16
- Peru 22 7
- Philippines 13 4
- South Korea 15 1

GREENLAND

ICELAND

NORWAY SWEDEN FINLAND

UNION OF SOVIET SOCIALIST REPUBLICS

IRELAND UNITED KINGDOM DENMARK
NETH. BEL. E GER POLAND
SWI. W GER CZECH
FRANCE AUSTRIA HUNGARY ROMANIA
YUGOSLAVIA
BULGARIA
PORTUGAL SPAIN ITALY ALB. GREECE TURKEY

MONGOLIA

CHINA

TUNISIA MALTA MOROCCO CYPRUS LEBANON SYRIA IRAQ IRAN AFGHANISTAN
ISRAEL JORDAN
WESTERN SAHARA ALGERIA LIBYA EGYPT KUW. BAHRAIN QATAR PAKISTAN NEPAL BHUTAN
SAUDI ARABIA UAE
MAURITANIA OMAN INDIA BURMA
CAPE VERDE MALI NIGER CHAD N YEMEN LAOS
SENEGAL SUDAN S YEMEN THAILAND
GAMBIA BURKINA DJIBOUTI
GUINEA BISSAU GUINEA NIGERIA PHILIPPINES
SIERRA LEONE IVORY BENIN CAR ETHIOPIA KAM VIETNAM
LIBERIA COAST GHANA TOGO CAMEROON SOMALIA SRI LANKA
SAO TOME & PRINCIPE GABON KENYA BRUNEI
EQUATORIAL GUINEA CONGO ZAIRE MALDIVES MALAYSIA
TANZANIA SINGAPORE
ANGOLA COMOROS
ZAMBIA MALAWI SEYCHELLES IN
NAMIBIA ZIMBABWE MOZAMBIQUE
BOTSWANA MADAGASCAR MAURITIUS
SOUTH AFRICA REUNION

## LAW AND REALITY

Age at marriage in India, early 1980s

21  18
9  11

legal age        most common age

## COUNTRY BRIDES

The number of rural women (aged 15-19) ever officially married for every 100 married women who live in towns (aged 15-19), late.1970s

- Bangladesh 130
- Colombia 192
- Indonesia 210
- Jamaica 117
- Jordan 181
- Malaysia 375
- Mexico 200
- Pakistan 150
- Philippines 200
- S. Korea 200
- Sri Lanka 117
- Thailand 213

Copyright © Pluto Press

Most women and men in the world spend most of their lives as married people, but for women this is a way of life.

Marriage grants women adult status. But many women marry while themselves still children. Early marriages bring many hardships, resulting in many more births, less autonomy, and a greater likelihood of being widowed in mid-life.

Even though legal age minimums for marriage are rising everywhere, youthful weddings still take place, because marrying-off adolescent daughters rids older parents of useless cargo; because in many places there is no role for a single woman in society; and because other older men value young wives – for their virginity and social status.

Women marry youngest in the country, where there are fewer opportunities for independence and change than in the city.

**PROPORTION OF WOMEN AGED 15-19 EVER OFFICIALLY MARRIED**
most recent year, *percentages*

- more than 50
- 25-49.9
- 10-24.9
- below 10
- unknown or unclear
- countries in which polygyny is practised

# SHELTERS: THE FIRST TEN YEARS

Year in which first women's shelter was opened

| 1972 | 1974 | 1976 | 1977 | 1978 | 1979 | 1980 | 1981 |
|------|------|------|------|------|------|------|------|
| UK, Canada | Netherlands, USA, Australia | West Germany | Sweden, Israel, Japan, South Africa | Austria | Finland | India, Mexico | Denmark, Thailand |

# SECOND BEST

The preference for sons or daughters, in 27 countries, 1980s

♂ son    ♀ daughter

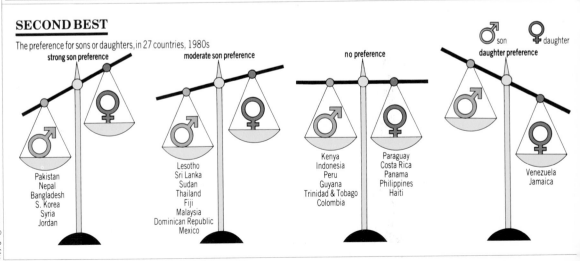

**strong son preference**

Pakistan
Nepal
Bangladesh
S. Korea
Syria
Jordan

**moderate son preference**

Lesotho
Sri Lanka
Sudan
Thailand
Fiji
Malaysia
Dominican Republic
Mexico

**no preference**

Kenya
Indonesia
Peru
Guyana
Trinidad & Tobago
Colombia

Paraguay
Costa Rica
Panama
Philippines
Haiti

**daughter preference**

Venezuela
Jamaica

Copyright © Pluto Press

# DOMESTIC DISORDERS 3

Men of all classes and countries use violence and coercion to 'keep women in their place'. Millions of women are beaten each year in their homes; many are killed. Some cultures encourage wife-beating as a man's right; in others, the problem is hidden away as a 'private' matter. There is little official recognition of this violence; but women throughout the world are organizing against it, and battered women's shelters now exist in many countries.

In Islamic states, the veiling and seclusion of women serve to keep them dependent on their husbands and exclusive to them. There is a current resurgence in the observance and enforcement of veiling practices; in two countries, the veil is compulsory for women in public.

Domestic coercion stems from the fact that in most countries women are considered to be men's property, and girls are less valued than boys.

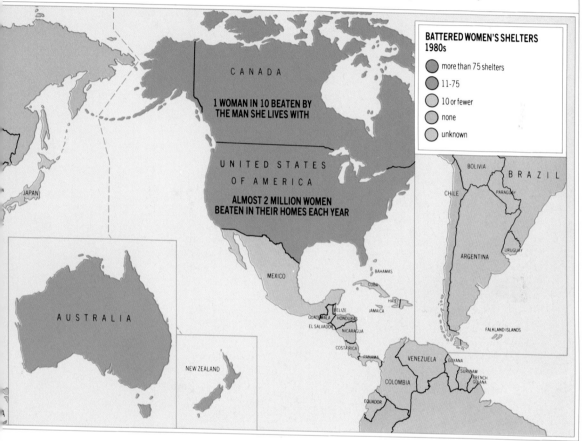

**BATTERED WOMEN'S SHELTERS 1980s**

- more than 75 shelters
- 11–75
- 10 or fewer
- none
- unknown

CANADA

**1 WOMAN IN 10 BEATEN BY THE MAN SHE LIVES WITH**

UNITED STATES OF AMERICA

**ALMOST 2 MILLION WOMEN BEATEN IN THEIR HOMES EACH YEAR**

## KEEPING WOMEN IN THEIR PLACE

Veiling of women in countries where over 50 per cent of the population is Muslim

- compulsory
- most women veiled
- some women veiled
- few women veiled
- other Islamic countries
- other countries
- seclusion is accepted practice

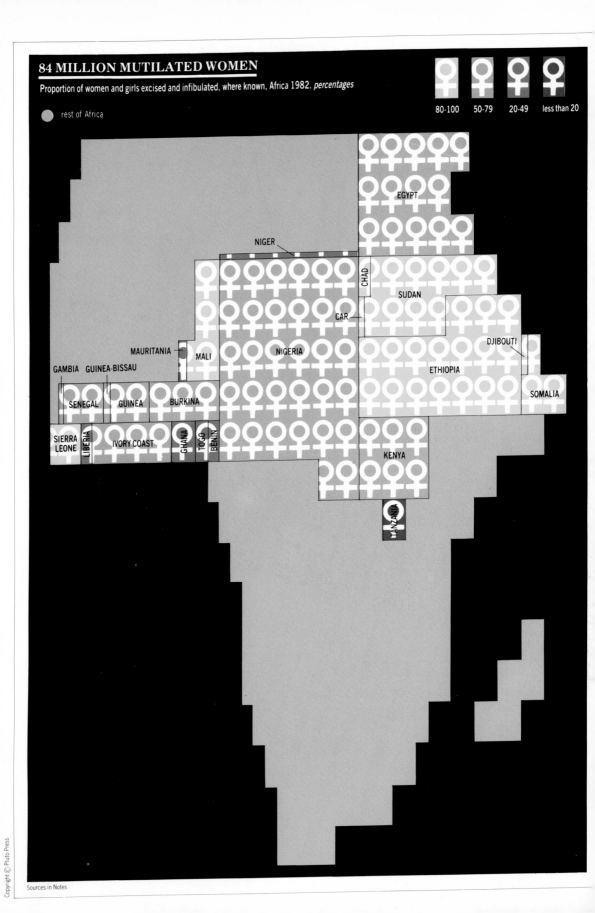

# 84 MILLION MUTILATED WOMEN

Proportion of women and girls excised and infibulated, where known, Africa 1982. *percentages*

80-100    50-79    20-49    less than 20

rest of Africa

EGYPT

NIGER

CHAD

SUDAN

MAURITANIA    MALI    CAR

DJIBOUTI

GAMBIA    GUINEA-BISSAU    NIGERIA

ETHIOPIA

SENEGAL    GUINEA    BURKINA    SOMALIA

SIERRA LEONE    LIBERIA    IVORY COAST    GHANA    TOGO    BENIN

KENYA

TANZANIA

Copyright © Pluto Press

Sources in Notes

Female genital mutilation – female circumcision as it is sometimes called – is extensively practised in Africa and the Middle East. It may be performed by older village women on babies as young as a few days old or on girls in their late adolescence. The 'operation' is rarely performed with surgical tools or skill any knowledge of anatomy or the use of anaesthesia.

Reasons given for the operation are varied, but wherever it is practised, it prepares girls for marriage by helping to ensure their premarital purity. It lessens sexual desire, and so reduces the temptation for girls and women to have intercourse before marriage – very important where virginity is an absolute prerequisite for a bride-to-be.

Genital mutilation is justified in other ways too. Some Moslem groups believe it is demanded by the Islamic faith (and only Moslems practise infibulation). Other groups hold erroneous beliefs about human biology and use circumcision as contraception. In some cultures, female genitals are considered unclean, and circumcision serves literally to smooth and ritually purify them.

Genital mutilation has staggering physical and mental health consequences for women. Infections (frequently fatal), haemorrhage, and other extreme long-term physical complications, are common. The extent and degree of sexual and mental health problems can only be guessed at, though, because circumcised women are often hesitant to discuss a subject that means little to them or is embarrassing: their sexuality. In spite of growing worldwide concern about genital mutilation, the practice is not yet declining.

Female circumcision is practised in the West, sometimes surreptitiously, but occurrences are sporadic and undocumented.

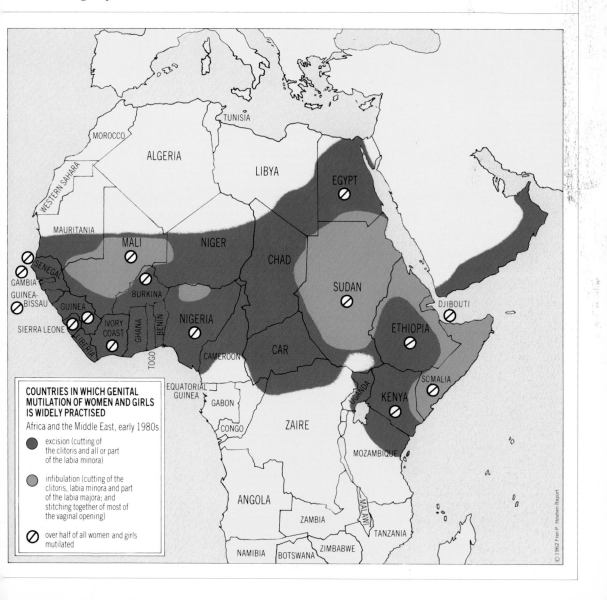

**COUNTRIES IN WHICH GENITAL MUTILATION OF WOMEN AND GIRLS IS WIDELY PRACTISED**

Africa and the Middle East, early 1980s

- excision (cutting of the clitoris and all or part of the labia minora)
- infibulation (cutting of the clitoris, labia minora and part of the labia majora; and stitching together of most of the vaginal opening)
- ⊘ over half of all women and girls mutilated

© 1962 Fran P. Hosken Report

# MANY MARRIAGES BREAK UP

The number of marriages ending in divorce

**USA 1980** 1 in 2

**USSR 1981** 1 in 3 (unofficial)

Annual average number of divorces for every 1,000 married couples, where known, most recent year

USA **over 2**

Australia, Egypt, Libya, Sweden, UK **10.1 - 2**

Canada, Czechoslovakia, Finland, Hungary **7.6 - 1**

West Germany, Romania, Tunisia, Uruguay, Venezuela **5.1 - 7.**

Bulgaria, France, Iran, Iraq, Israel, Japan, Poland, Singapore **2.6 -**

Costa Rica, Ecuador, Guatemala, Italy, S. Korea, Sri Lanka **below 2.**

## UNMARRIED WOMEN

Proportion of women's reproductive life (15-49) spent unmarried, early 1980s, *percentages*

- never married
- separated/divorced
- widowed

Bangladesh  5  3  11
Colombia  28  8  3
Jordan  20  1  4
Kenya  14  4  4
Philippines  30  1  2

Copyright © Pluto Press

Women marry for a variety of reasons: economic security, social status, and emotional wellbeing. But women who don't marry are often viewed as failures, even pariahs, and frequently see themselves that way.

Worst off by far are women once married, now single. The social status of widows and divorcees can be very low. In some cultures, widows are not even allowed to remarry; thus losing their one possible route back to security.

Divorce is not a universal right for men, much less for women. In most Muslim countries, a man can divorce simply by declaring his intentions, while his wife has no right to divorce at all.

Divorce is a mixed blessing for women: this important right can leave women and children worse off financially, while their ex-husbands gain. Divorce is increasing worldwide – for better or for worse.

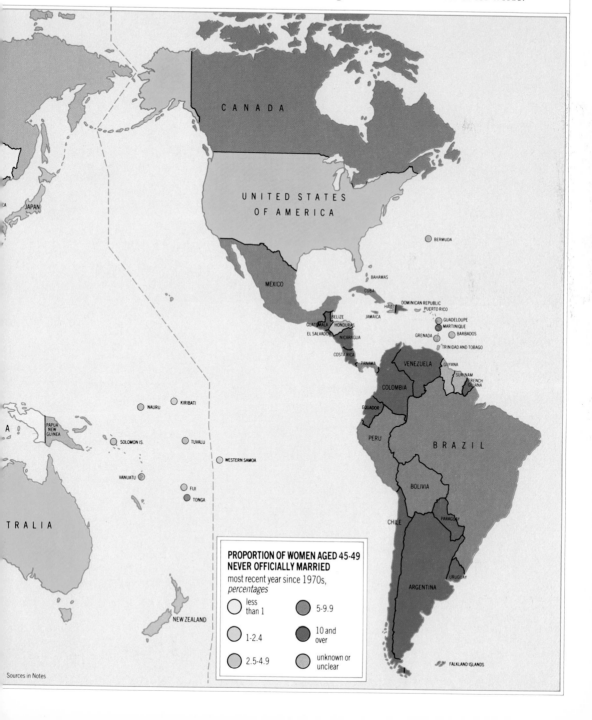

**PROPORTION OF WOMEN AGED 45-49 NEVER OFFICIALLY MARRIED**

most recent year since 1970s, *percentages*

- less than 1
- 1-2.4
- 2.5-4.9
- 5-9.9
- 10 and over
- unknown or unclear

Sources in Notes

# MANY WAYS TO BE MOTHERS

Births to mothers who are single or in a union other than 'official marriage' as a proportion of all births, Caribbean, where known, early 1980s, *percentages*

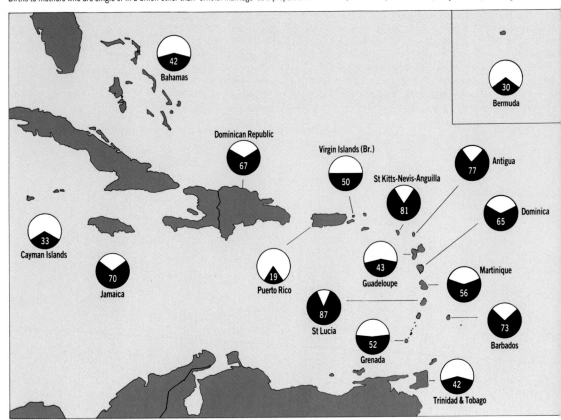

# TEENAGE MOTHERS

Births to women under 20 years old as a proportion of all births, latest available year since 1970s, *percentages*

over 20  11-20  5-10  below 5  unknown or unclear

Copyright © Pluto Press

Childbirth is one of the few true universals in women's lives. Women are the ones who bear children, a fact that is used everywhere to construct theories and institutions which define, limit, and dictate their roles in society.

But the conditions of pregnancy and motherhood vary widely. In some countries, women have an average of seven children; in others, fewer than two. This is the result of different population policies,

varying standards of health and wealth, differing pressures from men who often see their manhood affirmed by the number of children they father, and the degree of autonomy accorded to women.

Many teenage women have children – as young brides, or as single mothers. Many women, in some places the majority, have children when single or in consensual unions. Official marital status has little influence on women's childbearing experiences.

## TOTAL FERTILITY RATE

Average number of children women bear, early 1980s
extremes: West Germany 1.4 - Kenya, Zimbabwe above 8.0

○ below 2   ◔ 2.0-4.0   ◑ 4.1-6.0   ● above 6   ○ unknown or unclear

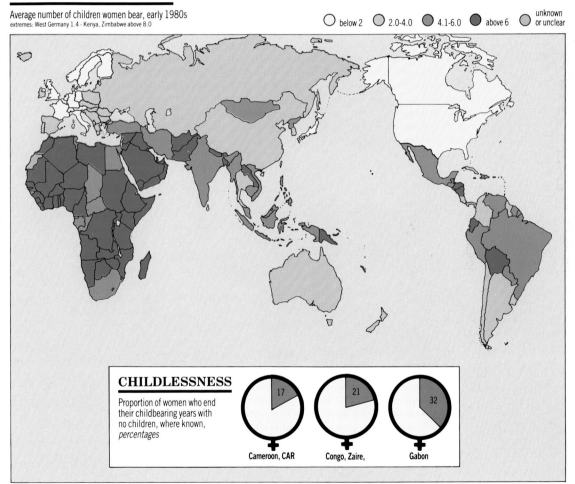

### CHILDLESSNESS

Proportion of women who end their childbearing years with no children, where known, *percentages*

17 — Cameroon, CAR

21 — Congo, Zaire,

32 — Gabon

## TEST-TUBE BABIES

| Use of in-vitro fertilization, mid-1985 | first practised | babies born number | centres number | | first practised | babies born number | centres number |
|---|---|---|---|---|---|---|---|
| UK | 1978 | over 200 | 8 | Japan | 1982 | 20-30 | over 10 |
| France | 1978 | 100-200 | over 60 | Denmark | 1982 | 1 | 2-3 |
| Australia | 1979 | over 200 | 10 | Sweden | 1982-83 | 8 | 4 |
| USA | 1980 | about 180 | about 108 | Switzerland | 1982-83 | 2 | (public) 7 |
| West Germany | 1982 | 130 | 19 | Israel | 1983 | 6-8 | 4-6 |
| Brazil | 1982 | 2-3 | 6 | Netherlands | 1983 | 20 | 8 |

Sources in Notes

# PUTTING MONEY WHERE THE MOUTH IS

Cents or fractions of a cent spent on family planning out of every dollar the central government spends, selected examples, most recent year since 1976

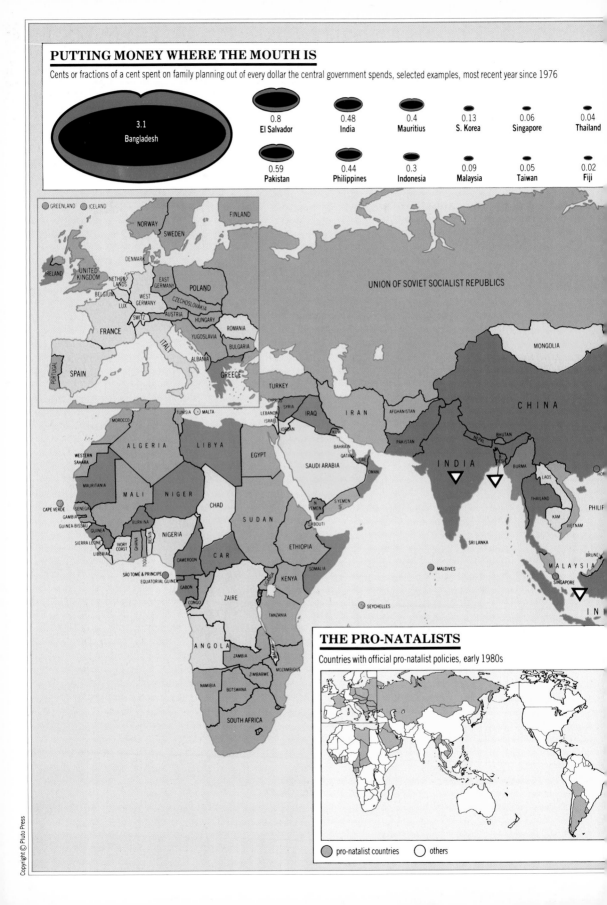

| | | | | | |
|---|---|---|---|---|---|
| 3.1 Bangladesh | | | | | |
| 0.8 El Salvador | 0.48 India | 0.4 Mauritius | 0.13 S. Korea | 0.06 Singapore | 0.04 Thailand |
| 0.59 Pakistan | 0.44 Philippines | 0.3 Indonesia | 0.09 Malaysia | 0.05 Taiwan | 0.02 Fiji |

## THE PRO-NATALISTS

Countries with official pro-natalist policies, early 1980s

pro-natalist countries    others

Copyright © Pluto Press

Most governments support some family planning: some subsidize contraceptive supplies, others give tax relief to smaller families. But everywhere, such resources fall far short of demand and millions of women have no family planning support. Funding commitments are a good indicator of actual government support.

Government involvement in family planning is not always beneficial. Some governments wield population-control policies with little regard for women's rights or health. Coercive sterilization, especially of poorer women and women from ethnic minority groups, is sometimes used to effect a quick reduction in population growth.

Pro-natalist governments want to increase population, often to ensure the continued supply of military manpower; this is sometimes accomplished by denying women family planning services.

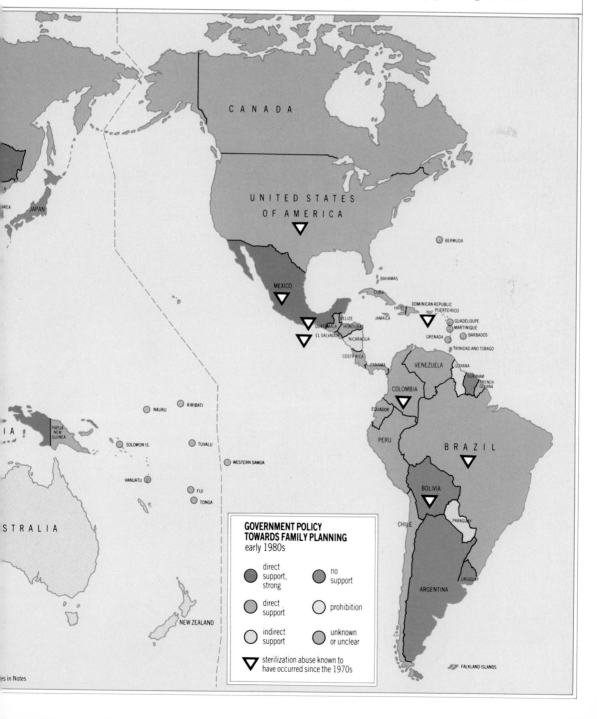

**GOVERNMENT POLICY
TOWARDS FAMILY PLANNING**
early 1980s

- direct support, strong
- direct support
- indirect support
- no support
- prohibition
- unknown or unclear

▽ sterilization abuse known to have occurred since the 1970s

# SPENDING ON RESEARCH AND DEVELOPMENT

Decline in private investment in contraceptive research, *percentages*

Public spending, 1978, *percentages*

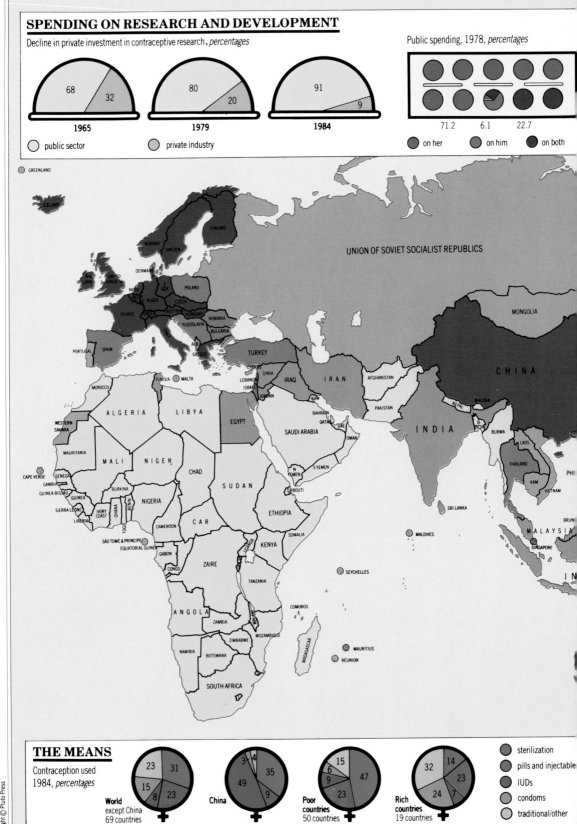

**1965**  68  32

**1979**  80  20

**1984**  91  9

○ public sector  ○ private industry

71.2  6.1  22.7

● on her  ● on him  ● on both

## THE MEANS

Contraception used
1984, *percentages*

**World**
except China
69 countries
23  31  15  8  23

**China**
3  4  35  49  9

**Poor countries**
50 countries
15  6  9  23  47

**Rich countries**
19 countries
32  14  23  7  24

● sterilization
● pills and injectable
● IUDs
● condoms
● traditional/other

Copyright © Pluto Press

Most women are expected to exercise some control over the number of children they bear. But what seems to be a personal choice of contraceptive methods is strongly influenced by many factors over which women have little control: national population policies (see 7. *Population Policies*), international contraceptive-aid policies, religious taboos, the dominant role of men in family decision-making, and the economics of the production and distribution of contraceptives. Wealthy women, women in wealthy countries, and urban women generally have the best access to contraceptive services.

Private industry has largely withdrawn from research into contraception in order to avoid legal liability for faulty or dangerous products. Research is now mostly paid for by governments.

Little research money goes into the development of male contraceptives.

**MARRIED WOMEN AGED 15-44 USING CONTRACEPTION**
most recent year, *percentages*

- under 15%
- 15 - 39%
- 40 - 59%
- 60% and over
- unknown or unclear

Range: Angola, Benin, Burkina, Burundi, Cameroon, Chad, Ethiopia, Gambia, Guinea, Guinea-Bissau, Liberia, Malawi, Mali, Mauritania, Niger, Somalia, Zaire, Zambia, all 1% - France, 82%.

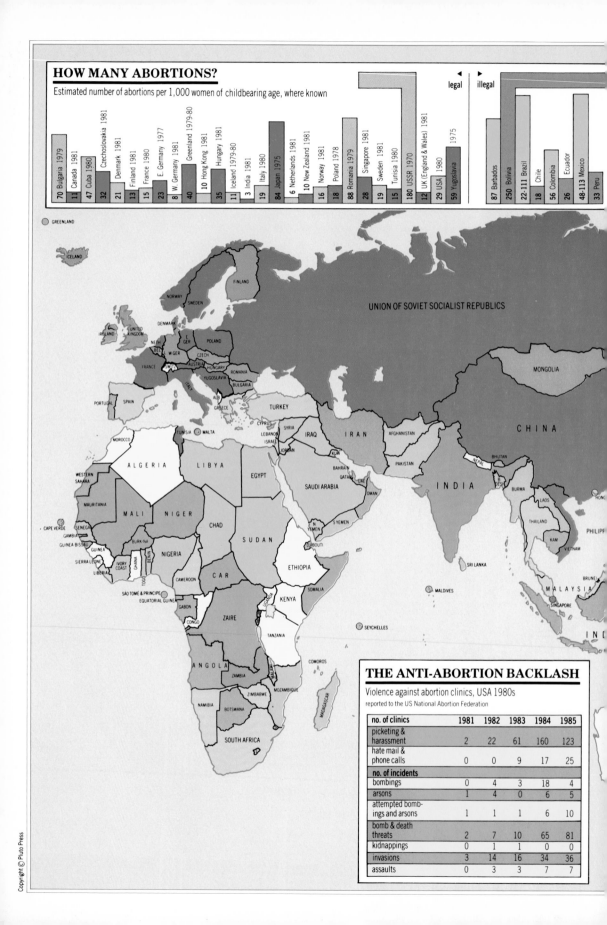

# HOW MANY ABORTIONS?

Estimated number of abortions per 1,000 women of childbearing age, where known

legal ◄ ► illegal

| | |
|---|---|
| 70 Bulgaria 1979 | |
| 11 Canada 1981 | |
| 47 Cuba 1980 | |
| 32 Czechoslovakia 1981 | |
| 21 Denmark 1981 | |
| 13 Finland 1981 | |
| 15 France 1980 | |
| 23 E. Germany 1977 | |
| 8 W. Germany 1981 | |
| 40 Greenland 1979-80 | |
| 10 Hong Kong 1981 | |
| 35 Hungary 1981 | |
| 11 Iceland 1979-80 | |
| 3 India 1981 | |
| 19 Italy 1980 | |
| 84 Japan 1975 | |
| 6 Netherlands 1981 | |
| 10 New Zealand 1981 | |
| 16 Norway 1981 | |
| 18 Poland 1978 | |
| 88 Romania 1979 | |
| 28 Singapore 1981 | |
| 19 Sweden 1981 | |
| 15 Tunisia 1980 | |
| 180 USSR 1970 | |
| 12 UK (England & Wales) 1981 | |
| 29 USA 1980 | |
| 59 Yugoslavia 1975 | |
| 87 Barbados | |
| 250 Bolivia | |
| 22-111 Brazil | |
| 18 Chile | |
| 56 Colombia | |
| 26 Ecuador | |
| 48-113 Mexico | |
| 33 Peru | |

## THE ANTI-ABORTION BACKLASH

Violence against abortion clinics, USA 1980s
reported to the US National Abortion Federation

| no. of clinics | 1981 | 1982 | 1983 | 1984 | 1985 |
|---|---|---|---|---|---|
| picketing & harassment | 2 | 22 | 61 | 160 | 123 |
| hate mail & phone calls | 0 | 0 | 9 | 17 | 25 |
| **no. of incidents** | | | | | |
| bombings | 0 | 4 | 3 | 18 | 4 |
| arsons | 1 | 4 | 0 | 6 | 5 |
| attempted bombings and arsons | 1 | 1 | 1 | 6 | 10 |
| bomb & death threats | 2 | 7 | 10 | 65 | 81 |
| kidnappings | 0 | 1 | 1 | 0 | 0 |
| invasions | 3 | 14 | 16 | 34 | 36 |
| assaults | 0 | 3 | 3 | 7 | 7 |

Copyright © Pluto Press

Abortion is an old and common form of birth control. The past two decades have seen a liberalizing trend in abortion laws.

Legal abortion gives women the right to control their own bodies, and helps them avoid the health risks of 'back-street' operations, giving poor women access to what rich women have always had. Abortion has also been used to promote government population policies.

But even in 'legal' countries, women often cannot afford, get access to, or get away with abortion. And in 'illegal' countries, abortions are still performed: by unskilled people under unclean conditions, resulting in death and disease among desperate women.

Opponents of abortion argue on religious, moral and even political grounds. Emotions run high where abortion is a matter of public debate, and the backlash has sometimes taken violent forms.

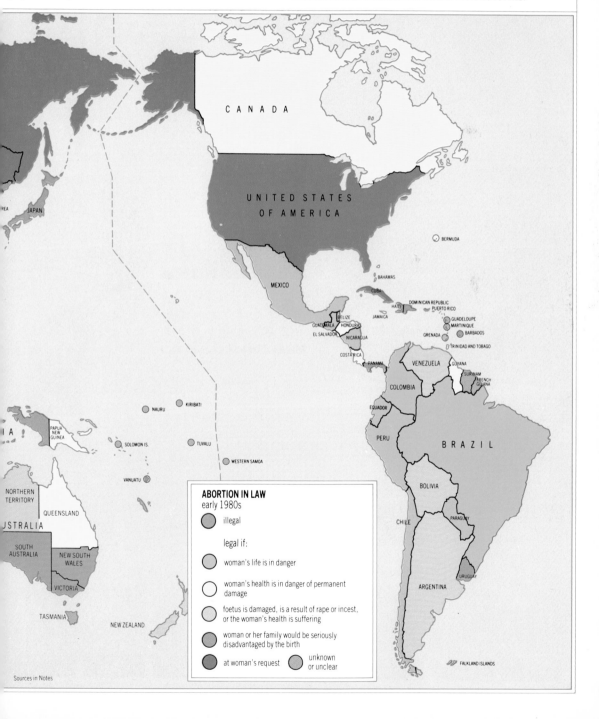

**ABORTION IN LAW**
early 1980s

- illegal

legal if:

- woman's life is in danger
- woman's health is in danger of permanent damage
- foetus is damaged, is a result of rape or incest, or the woman's health is suffering
- woman or her family would be seriously disadvantaged by the birth
- at woman's request
- unknown or unclear

Sources in Notes

# INFANT MORTALITY IN A DIVIDED WORLD

Infant deaths per 1,000 live births, most recent year since 1979

101 and above | 51-100 | 26-50 | 25 or under | unknown or unclear

rich

poor

rich

NEW ZEALAND

poor

## GRAVEYARDS FOR THE WORLD'S CHILDREN

Share of deaths of children below 1 year old
1975-80 *percentages*  world 100 per cent

India 27.6

China 9.3

Bangladesh 5.0

Nigeria 4.7

Indonesia 4.4

Pakistan 4.3

Brazil 2.9

Ethiopia 2.1

Vietnam 2.0

Turkey 1.8

Iran 1.7

Egypt 1.6

Afghanistan 1.4

Mexico 1.4

Zaire 1.3

Burma 1.3

South Africa 1.0

Algeria 1.0

Sudan 1.0

Philippines 0.9

poor

rich

poor

rich

JAPAN

# MATERNAL MORTALITY IN A DIVIDED WORLD

Deaths of mothers per 100,000 live births, 1970s

101 and above | 51-100 | 26-50 | 25 or under | unknown or unclear

# EDUCATION AND INFANT MORTALITY

The more educated the mother, the less likely is death in infancy.
Deaths in the first two years of life per 1,000 children, Latin America, early 1970s

number of infant deaths

number of years mother spent at school: 0 | 1-3 | 4-6 | 7-9 | 10+

**Argentina:** 96, 75, 59, 39, 26
**Colombia:** 126, 95, 63, 42, 32
**Costa Rica:** 125, 98, 70, 51, 33
**Ecuador:** 176, 134, 101, 61, 46
**El Salvador:** 158, 142, 111, 58, 30
**Guatemala:** 169, 135, 85, 58, 44
**Honduras:** 171, 129, 99, 60, 35
**Peru:** 207, 136, 102, 77, 70

Copyright © Pluto Press

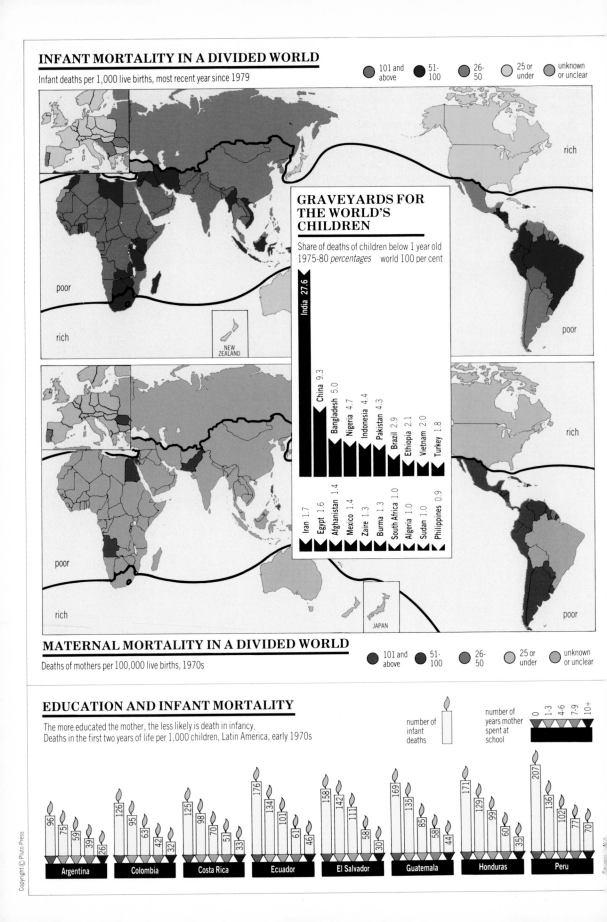

Pregnancy and childbirth are major causes of death for women and children in all of the world's poorer countries. These countries constitute a recognized danger zone for childbearing women and their children. But even in the world's richest countries, maternal and infant mortality rates can be almost as high – for poor women and women from ethnic minorities. Everywhere, high death rates are associated with early marriage and childbearing (see 2. *Young Brides*), and with low levels of education for women.

The preference for boys throughout much of the world means that girls sometimes suffer severe neglect; this is reflected in patterns of child mortality. Girls are biologically stronger than boys at birth; in early infancy, their death rates are lower. But the balance shifts in early childhood, when death rates for girls surpass those for boys.

## THE ODDS CHANGE

Numbers of girls who die, for every 100 boys who die, below 1 year-old and 1-4 years old — selected examples, most recent year since 1975

Bangladesh 100 / 112 / 93; Barbados 100 / 200 / 91; Ecuador 100 / 105 / 89; Egypt 100 / 122 / 100; India 100 / 300 / 109; Malta 100 / 133 / 52; Nepal 100 / 110 / 97; Pakistan 100 / 126 / 89; Panama 100 / 109 / 86; Peru 100 / 102 / 89; S. Korea 100 / 105 / 86; Uruguay 100 / 106 / 81

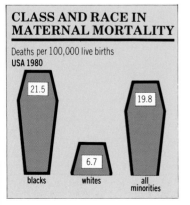

## CLASS AND RACE IN MATERNAL MORTALITY

Deaths per 100,000 live births — USA 1980: blacks 21.5, whites 6.7, all minorities 19.8

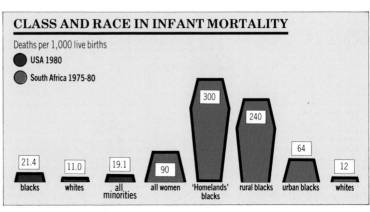

## CLASS AND RACE IN INFANT MORTALITY

Deaths per 1,000 live births — USA 1980; South Africa 1975-80: blacks 21.4, whites 11.0, all minorities 19.1, all women 90, 'Homelands' blacks 300, rural blacks 240, urban blacks 64, whites 12

Sources in Notes

# WHITE COATS

Doctors and midwives (including traditional birth attendants) per 10,000 population, selected examples, early 1980s

doctors ⬜ midwives

| Columbia | France | Hong Kong | Hungary | India | Kenya | Philippines | Spain | Sudan | Syria | Thailand | UK |
|---|---|---|---|---|---|---|---|---|---|---|---|
| 4.7 6.0 | 16.6 / 1.8 | 6.3 / 14.2 | 25.0 / 2.4 | 2.5 / 9.3 | 0.6 / 12.0 | 3.2 / 8.0 | 20.0 / 1.2 | 0.8 / 7.6 | 4.0 / 1.4 | 1.3 / 7.1 | 16.6 / 4.5 |

## SUPPORT IN LABOUR

Number of midwives practising, Western Europe, early 1980s

- number of midwives practising
- relative size of population

| UK | West Germany | France | Spain | Netherlands | Belgium | Sweden | Finland |
|---|---|---|---|---|---|---|---|
| 20,698 | 5,566 | 8,899 | 4,489 | 874 | 1,178 | 3,540 | 887 |

Midwives and traditional birth attendants deliver most of the world's babies. They are the primary source of health care and advice for most women during pregnancy, birth, and early childcare. 'Modern medicine' serves only a wealthier minority in the world, and is seldom available to rural women or the urban poor.

Until recently, most governments ignored or legislated against traditional birth attendants. Now, increasingly, they are being recognized as important primary health care providers, and they are being given medical training. But progress is slow, and the World Health Organization estimates that two-thirds of women in poor countries have no access to a trained health worker.

In rich countries, growing disenchantment with modern medicine's approach to birth care is leading to a resurgence of midwifery.

**PROPORTION OF BIRTHS ATTENDED BY MEDICALLY-TRAINED PERSONNEL**
where known, early 1980s, *percentages*

- below 30
- 31-50
- 51-70
- 71-90
- above 90
- unknown or unclear

# HOMEWORK

The number of people per household, world, early 1980s, *percentages*

less than 3 | 3-3.9 | 4-4.9 | 5-5.9 | 6 or mo[re]

◄————— world population: about 4,500 million ————————►

| 12% | 9% | 41% | 36% | 2[%] |

46% of these in USA | 30% of these in Japan | 59% of these in China | 45% of these in India | 29% of thes[e] in Algeria

GREENLAND

ICELAND

FINLAND

NORWAY
SWEDEN

DENMARK
IRELAND  UNITED KINGDOM
NETH  E GER
BEL  W GER  POLAND
FRANCE  LUX  CZECH
AUSTRIA  HUNGARY
SWITZ  ROMANIA
YUGOSLAVIA
ITALY  BULGARIA

UNION OF SOVIET SOCIALIST REPUBLICS

PORTUGAL  SPAIN
ALB
GREECE  TURKEY
CYPRUS

MONGOLIA

MOROCCO
TUNISIA  MALTA
SYRIA  IRAQ  IRAN  AFGHANISTAN
LEBANON  JORDAN
ISRAEL
KUW
PAKISTAN

CHINA

WESTERN SAHARA
ALGERIA  LIBYA  EGYPT
SAUDI ARABIA
BAHRAIN
QATAR
UAE
OMAN

NEPAL  BHUTAN
BANG
INDIA  BURMA

MAURITANIA
MALI  NIGER  CHAD
N YEMEN  S YEMEN

CAPE VERDE
SENEGAL
GAMBIA
GUINEA BISSAU  GUINEA  BURKINA
SIERRA LEONE  IVORY COAST  GHANA  BENIN
LIBERIA  TOGO
NIGERIA
SUDAN
DJIBOUTI
ETHIOPIA
SOMALIA

LAOS
THAILAND
KAM  VIETNAM

PH

SÃO TOMÉ & PRINCIPE
EQUATORIAL GUINEA
CAMEROON  CAR
GABON  CONGO
ZAIRE

MALDIVES

MALAYSIA
BRUN
SINGAPORE

UGANDA  KENYA
TANZANIA

SEYCHELLES

IN

ANGOLA
ZAMBIA
ZIMBABWE
MOZAMBIQUE
NAMIBIA  BOTSWANA

COMOROS
MADAGASCAR
MAURITIUS
RÉUNION

SRI LANKA

SOUTH AFRICA

# CHILD CARE

Proportion of pre-school children in day care centres, latest year since 1978, *percentages*

 37 Sweden  30 Norway  25 China  24 Bulgaria  15 USA  14 Canada  8 Yugoslavia  6 Kenya  6 Tanzania  <1 Nicaragua  Botswana

Copyright © Pluto Press

Families and households are created and maintained almost entirely by women's labour. Many women, starting as young brides, spend their entire lives caring for them. There are a number of reasons, especially in poor countries, for having large families – they provide social security and a labour supply, for example. But families with many dependent children also place excessive demands on women's daily labour.

Worldwide, the nuclear family is replacing extended family living, and global trends are toward smaller families; but it is still true that one-third of the world's population live in households of five or more people.

Childcare accounts for the largest share of women's household labour – and limits their ability to take paid work outside the home. In only a few countries are there alternative childcare facilities.

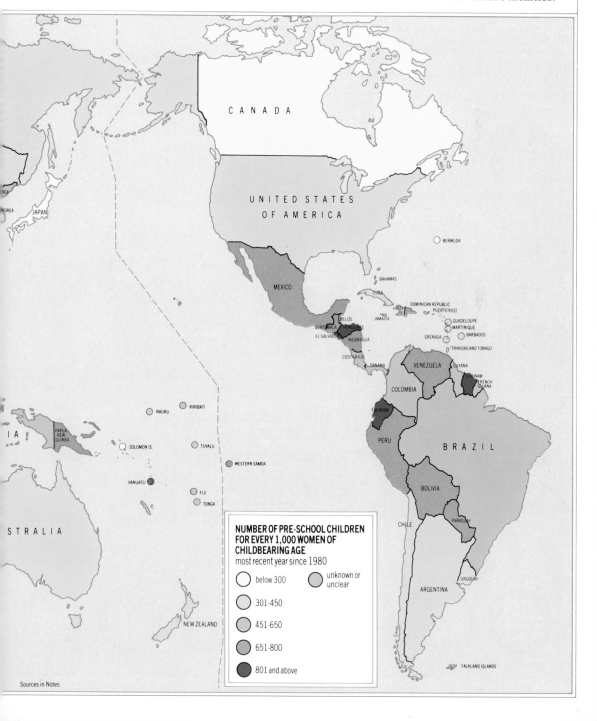

**NUMBER OF PRE-SCHOOL CHILDREN FOR EVERY 1,000 WOMEN OF CHILDBEARING AGE**
most recent year since 1980

○ below 300

○ unknown or unclear

○ 301-450

○ 451-650

○ 651-800

● 801 and above

Sources in Notes

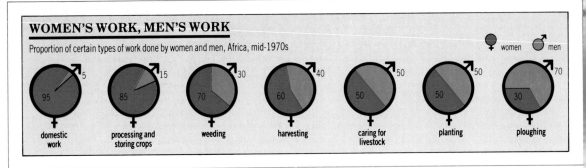

# WOMEN'S WORK, MEN'S WORK

Proportion of certain types of work done by women and men, Africa, mid-1970s

women    men

| domestic work | processing and storing crops | weeding | harvesting | caring for livestock | planting | ploughing |
| 95 / 5 | 85 / 15 | 70 / 30 | 60 / 40 | 50 / 50 | 50 / 50 | 30 / 70 |

# UNSYNCHRONIZED CLOCKS

The number of hours spent by men for every 100 hours spent by women on certain activities, most recent year 1970s and 1980s

women    men

### HOUSEHOLD TASKS

women

| 100 hours | 12 industrial countries *employed men compared with employed women* | USA *unmarried men compared with unmarried women* | USSR *all* | Czechoslovakia *all* | Hungary *all* | Burkina *all* |
|---|---|---|---|---|---|---|
| 100 hours | 32 | 51 | 42 | 29 | 58 | 4 |

### LEISURE

| | 12 industrial countries | USA | USSR | Czechoslovakia | Hungary | Burkina |
|---|---|---|---|---|---|---|

women

| 100 hours | 140 | 141 | 161 | 144 | 136 | 150 |

### PAID WORK

| | 12 industrial countries | USA | USSR | Czechoslovakia | Hungary | Austria |
|---|---|---|---|---|---|---|

women

| 100 hours | 119 | 103 | 103 | 113 | 127 | 137 |

Copyright © Pluto Press

Women work longer hours than men do. Women do the household chores and take care of the children. They tend the goats, till the family garden, collect water, gather firewood.

Women are also entering the paid workforce in increasing numbers, but no one is taking over at home. Busy, fatigued mothers cannot pursue training or education that might help develop their self-sufficiency or alleviate drudgery. Only one side of the traditional division of labour is breaking down and only three countries in the world have made the sharing of housework official public policy.

Women everywhere get little financial or social recognition for working more, resting less, and doing a greater variety of work than men. Their work is often statistically invisible: it is estimated that the official enumerators count only about two-thirds of women's work.

## NIGHT AND DAY

Proportion of the day typically spent by women on certain activities, selected countries, most recent year from 1970s and 1980s, *percentages*

- household, including family care, supplies, cleaning
- paid work, including work-related travel
- self-maintenance, including sleep and other physiological necessities, and leisure

* Belgium, Bulgaria, Czechoslovakia, France, West Germany, East Germany, Hungary, Peru, Poland, USA, USSR, Yugoslavia excluding purely agricultural households.

# BEASTS OF BURDEN

Proportions of women agricultural workers by job status, Europe where data is known, 1980s, *percentages*

unpaid family workers
employees
employers

| Country | | | |
|---|---|---|---|
| Austria | 7 | | 38 |
| Belgium | 32 | 37 | 30 |
| Czechoslovakia | 62 | | 38 |
| Denmark | 73 | 19 | 7 |
| W. Germany | 80 | 11 | 9 |
| Greece | 60 | 2 | 38 |
| Netherlands | 61 | 21 | 18 |
| Spain | 57 | 13 | 31 |
| Sweden | 17 | 31 | 52 |
| Yugoslavia | 57 | 6 | 37 |

# FIELD WORK

Women working in agriculture as a proportion of all working women, countries with over 50 million population, most recent year from 1975, *percentages*

Mexico 0.3
USA 0.4
UK 1.0
West Germany 5.0
France 8.0
Italy 14.0
Brazil 17.0
Japan 18.0
Philippines 28.2
Indonesia 61.0
Bangladesh 69.8
Pakistan 70.0
India 82.6

Copyright © Pluto Press

Women produce at least half the world's output of food, mostly in poor, agricultural countries where they grow, harvest and prepare virtually all the food consumed by their families. In Africa they perform 60 to 80 per cent of agricultural work.

In Asia and Africa, almost all women who are employed work in agriculture: in Mozambique, for example, 90 per cent of working women are engaged in the production of food.

Because much of women's agricultural work is done in or near the home, is small in scale, part-time or seasonal, it is considered unimportant by official agencies. As a result, women are often left out of economic development schemes.

Women are at the bottom of the pay and power scales in agriculture: they are employees, not employers; unpaid sowers, reapers and breadmakers; not breadwinners on the human 'family farm'.

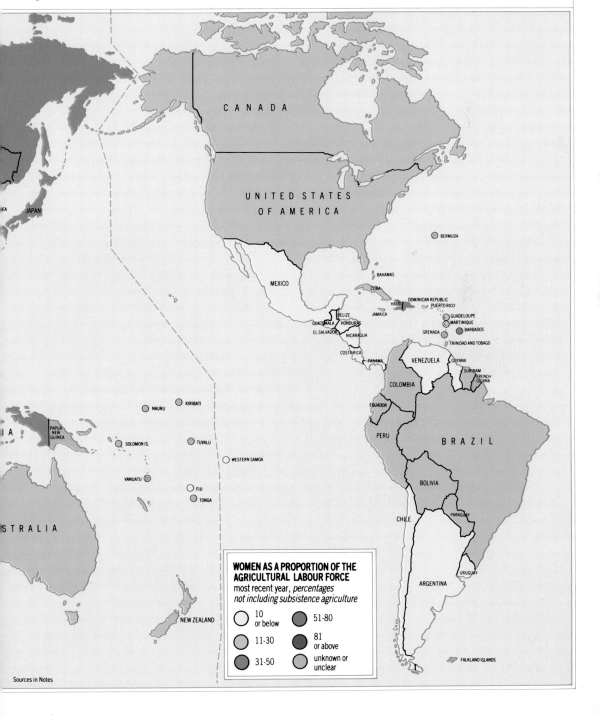

**WOMEN AS A PROPORTION OF THE AGRICULTURAL LABOUR FORCE**
most recent year, *percentages not including subsistence agriculture*

- 10 or below
- 11-30
- 31-50
- 51-80
- 81 or above
- unknown or unclear

Sources in Notes

Copyright © Pluto Press

# TIME TRENDS

Changes in women's share of the paid labour force, 1950-80, *percentages*

● 1950  ● 198█

| | | | | | | | | |
|---|---|---|---|---|---|---|---|---|
| **+4** | **+7** | **+6** | **+5** | **+4** | **+4** | **+3** | | |
| 31  35 | 26  33 | 28  34 | 18  23 | 53  57 | 30  34 | 30  33 | 33  32 | 64  60 |
| | | | | | | | −1 | −4 |
| **World** | **Oceania** | **North America** | **Latin America** | **Eastern Europe** | **Asia** | **Western Europe** | **Africa** | **USSR** |

GREENLAND
ICELAND
FINLAND
NORWAY
SWEDEN
DENMARK
IRELAND  UNITED KINGDOM
NETH
BEL  E GER
W GER  POLAND
FRANCE  CZECH
SWITZ  AUSTRIA  HUNGARY
ITALY  YUGOSLAVIA  ROMANIA
BULGARIA
PORTUGAL  SPAIN  ALB
GREECE  TURKEY

UNION OF SOVIET SOCIALIST REPUBLICS

MONGOLIA

CHINA

TUNISIA  MALTA
MOROCCO
CYPRUS  SYRIA
LEBANON  IRAQ  IRAN  AFGHANISTAN
ISRAEL
JORDAN
KUW  PAKISTAN
BAHRAIN
QATAR
UAE
OMAN

WESTERN SAHARA
ALGERIA  LIBYA  EGYPT
SAUDI ARABIA

MAURITANIA
MALI  NIGER  CHAD
SUDAN
N YEMEN  S YEMEN
DJIBOUTI

CAPE VERDE
GAMBIA  SENEGAL
GUINEA-BISSAU  GUINEA  BURKINA
SIERRA LEONE  IVORY  GHANA
COAST
LIBERIA  TOGO  BENIN
NIGERIA
CAMEROON
SÃO TOMÉ & PRINCIPE
EQUATORIAL GUINEA  GABON
CONGO  ZAIRE
CAR  ETHIOPIA
SOMALIA
KENYA
TANZANIA

ANGOLA
ZAMBIA
NAMIBIA  BOTSWANA  ZIMBABWE  MOZAMBIQUE

SOUTH AFRICA

NEPAL  BHUTAN
INDIA  BANG  BURMA
LAOS
THAILAND
KAM  VIETNAM
PHIL
SRI LANKA
MALDIVES
MALAYSIA
SINGAPORE
BRUNEI
SEYCHELLES
IN

# WOMANPOWER

Distribution of all women workers by region, 1975, *percentages*

WESTERN EUROPE 9
USSR & EASTERN EUROPE 15
NORTH AMERICA 7

EAST ASIA 31

AFRICA 9
SOUTH ASIA 25
LATIN AMERICA 4

OCEANIA <1

□ = 1%

Women represent about one-third of the paid labour force worldwide. This share is slowly growing in most places, with the largest increases occurring in industrializing countries. In two regions, women's labour force rates appear to have decreased over the past thirty years.

The picture of women's work that can be drawn from official labour force statistics, however, is unreliable and incomplete. It is widely understood that more women are working for wages, and at a greater rate of increase, than is revealed by these numbers. Increasingly, when women enter waged work, they do so in the 'informal' sector, as domestic servants and market traders, for example – labour that is often uncounted.

Several countries with unusually high records of women in the paid work force are also those with high rates of male emigration.

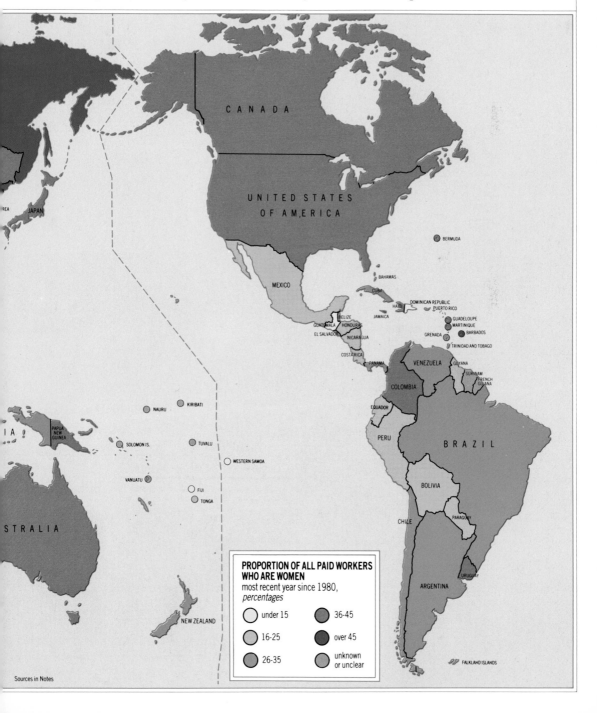

**PROPORTION OF ALL PAID WORKERS WHO ARE WOMEN**
most recent year since 1980, *percentages*

- under 15
- 16-25
- 26-35
- 36-45
- over 45
- unknown or unclear

Sources in Notes

# THE MARRIAGE FACTOR

The percentage of married women in paid work compared with the percentage of all women in paid work, selected examples, mid-1980s

married women    all women

| USA | Denmark | UK | Canada | France | West Germany | New Zealand | Italy | Netherlands | Ireland |
|---|---|---|---|---|---|---|---|---|---|
| 52 / 56 | 50 / 72 | 50 / 54 | 42 / 56 | 53 | 33 / 50 | 32 / 44 | 23 / 39 | 18 / 39 | 14 / 34 |

GREENLAND
ICELAND
NORWAY
SWEDEN
FINLAND
DENMARK
IRELAND
UNITED KINGDOM
NETH
BEL
E GER
POLAND
W GER
CZECH
FRANCE
SWITZ
AUSTRIA
HUNGARY
ROMANIA
YUGOSLAVIA
BULGARIA
ITALY
ALB
GREECE
PORTUGAL
SPAIN
UNION OF SOVIET SOCIALIST REPUBLICS
MONGOLIA
TUNISIA
MALTA
CYPRUS
SYRIA
LEBANON
ISRAEL
JORDAN
IRAQ
TURKEY
IRAN
AFGHANISTAN
CHINA
MOROCCO
ALGERIA
LIBYA
EGYPT
SAUDI ARABIA
KUW
BAHRAIN
QATAR
UAE
OMAN
PAKISTAN
NEPAL
BHUTAN
B'DESH
INDIA
BURMA
WESTERN SAHARA
MAURITANIA
MALI
NIGER
CHAD
SUDAN
N YEMEN
S YEMEN
LAOS
THAILAND
KAM
VIETNAM
PHILIP
CAPE VERDE
SENEGAL
GAMBIA
GUINEA-BISSAU
GUINEA
SIERRA LEONE
LIBERIA
IVORY COAST
BURKINA
GHANA
BENIN
TOGO
NIGERIA
CAMEROON
CAR
ETHIOPIA
DJIBOUTI
SOMALIA
SRI LANKA
MALDIVES
MALAYSIA
BRUNEI
SINGAPORE
SÃO TOME & PRINCIPE
EQUATORIAL GUINEA
GABON
CONGO
ZAIRE
UGANDA
KENYA
TANZANIA
SEYCHELLES
ANGOLA
ZAMBIA
MALAWI
MOZAMBIQUE
ZIMBABWE
NAMIBIA
BOTSWANA
SOUTH AFRICA

# CONTRARY DIRECTIONS

Proportions of women and men working for wages or in trade, selected examples, 1960-80, *percentages*

| | Sweden | Denmark | UK | Canada | France | USA | West Germany | Spain |
|---|---|---|---|---|---|---|---|---|
| 1960 men | 88 | 90 | 89 | 86 | 83 | 86 | 82 | 81 |
| 1960 women | 53 | 44 | 49 | 32 | 46 | 43 | 49 | 24 |
| 1980 women | 93 | 99 | 99 | 92 | 87 | 92 | 95 | 99 |
| 1980 men | 74 | 71 | 58 | 57 | 53 | 52 | 49 | 32 |

women    men    1960    1980

Copyright © Pluto Press

Most women who work outside the home do so because they have to – this is true whether the work is trading beans in a market, or typing in an office. Women's wages, increasingly, are essential for family survival. At the same time, women have primary responsibility for maintaining their families and households – work outside must be fitted around domestic duties. For many women, this means working a double day.

The proportion of women who work outside the home varies widely from country to country. Although more women are now working, in almost all cultures, there is resistance to it. This is especially true with regard to married women; men commonly feel it a dishonour for their wives to work. Employers often will not hire married women.

The strongest constraints on women being active outside the home exist in Islamic countries.

**PROPORTION OF WOMEN AGED 15 OR OVER, WORKING FOR WAGES OR TRADE**
most recent year since 1980

- over 65 per cent
- 46-65 per cent
- 26-45 per cent
- 11-25 per cent
- below 10 per cent
- unknown or unclear

World average: 42
Extremes: Guinea-Bissau, Qatar 2 – Burundi 95

# MEN ON THE MOVE

Countries where migration for work is predominantly male, 1980s

Botswana · Egypt · Lesotho · Mozambique · Sudan · Vietnam

Finland to Sweden

① Italy to Switzerland
② Italy to West Germany
③ Yugoslavia to West Germany
④ Yugoslavia to Switzerland
⑤ Greece to West Germany
⑥ Yugoslavia to Austria/Switzerland

UNION OF SOVIET SOCIALIST REPUBLICS

Portugal to France

Spain to France West Germany

Morocco to France

Algeria to France

Tunisia to France

Turkey to West Germany

Turkey to Netherlands/Austria/Sweden

India Bangladesh Pakistan Sri Lanka Malaysia to Western Europe

Sri Lanka to Middle East

Thailand to Western Europe

CHINA

MONGOLIA

INDIA

# FROM COUNTRY TO TOWN

Internal migration for work, 1980s

● men and women    ● predominantly women

rich

poor

rich

rich

poor

Copyright © Pluto Press

There is a huge rural to urban migration currently underway throughout the Third World. In some places, it is mostly the men who move to cities for work – sometimes never returning, and leaving in their wake a large population of poor, women-headed families (see 28. *Poverty*). In Latin America and parts of Asia, women outnumber men in the search for a new life and work in the cities.

Women also make up a large proportion of inter-national migrants, as part of families or on their own. Some migrant streams are created by em-ployers or governments recruiting 'cheap labour', such as the thousands of women brought from Sri Lanka to be domestic servants in the Middle East.

For many women, their new life is no better than the one they left behind, and may be worse. Migrant women are among the poorest of the poor, triply burdened by race, class and gender barriers.

India Bangladesh Pakistan Sri Lanka Malaysia to USA and Canada

Mexico to USA

Puerto Rico to USA

Caribbean to USA/Canada

Central America to USA/Canada

Colombia to Venezeula

Colombia to Ecuador

Bolivia to Argentina

Paraguay to Argentina

Chile to Argentina

Uruguay to Argentina

**FROM COUNTRY TO COUNTRY**
International migration for work, 1980s

**men and women**
major movement
significant movement

**predominantly women**
major movement
significant movement

Sources in Notes

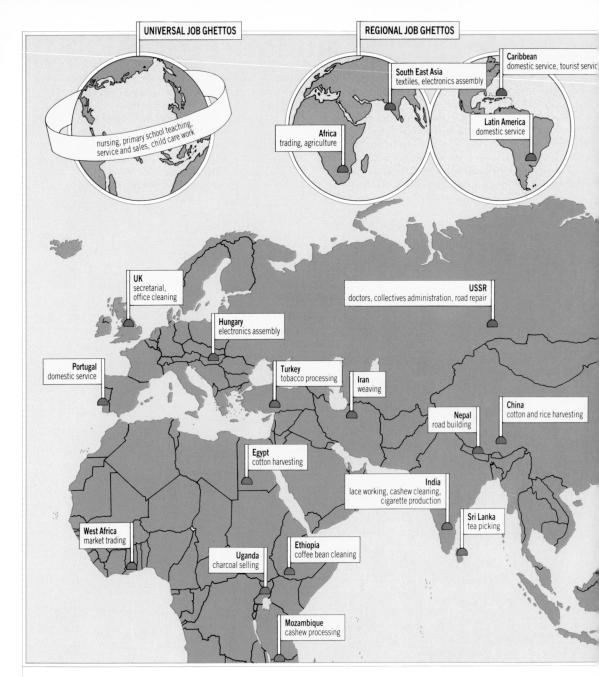

**UNIVERSAL JOB GHETTOS**

nursing, primary school teaching, service and sales, child care work

**REGIONAL JOB GHETTOS**

**South East Asia**
textiles, electronics assembly

**Caribbean**
domestic service, tourist servic

**Africa**
trading, agriculture

**Latin America**
domestic service

**UK**
secretarial, office cleaning

**USSR**
doctors, collectives administration, road repair

**Hungary**
electronics assembly

**Portugal**
domestic service

**Turkey**
tobacco processing

**Iran**
weaving

**China**
cotton and rice harvesting

**Nepal**
road building

**Egypt**
cotton harvesting

**India**
lace working, cashew cleaning, cigarette production

**Sri Lanka**
tea picking

**West Africa**
market trading

**Uganda**
charcoal selling

**Ethiopia**
coffee bean cleaning

**Mozambique**
cashew processing

## THREE JOB AREAS

Women as a proportion of waged workers, early 1980s, *percentages*

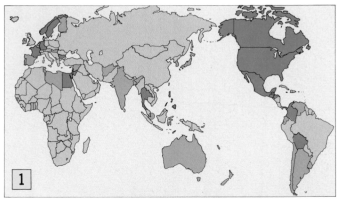

- 15 and below
- 46-60
- 16-30
- over 60
- 31-45
- unknown or unclear

**1** Administration and management

**2** Clerical work

**3** Manufacturing

Copyright © Pluto Press

The range of jobs that women fill in the workforce is much narrower than for men. And, in every country and every region of the world, there are jobs that are specifically defined as 'women's work'. These are the jobs that are filled almost exclusively by women – and are usually considered beneath men's station.

In some countries, almost all bank tellers and secretaries are women. In other countries, tea picking and cotton harvesting are considered women's work. In Latin America and the Caribbean, domestic service is almost entirely feminized, and up to 80 per cent of all women who earn wages work as servants. In South East Asia, textile manufacturing and electronics assembly rely heavily on female labour – and, especially, on a young, female workforce.

Although specifics vary, it is universally true that jobs defined as women's work carry low pay, low status, and little security: thus termed, 'job ghettos'.

**WOMEN'S WORK**
Jobs typically done by women, some examples, 1980s

**USA**
bank tellers, garment industry

**Mexico**
garment industry electronics assembly

**Guatemala**
crafts

**Nicaragua**
coffee picking

**Brazil**
market trading, teaching, textiles

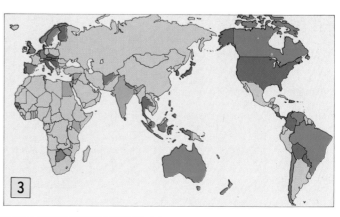

3

Sources in Notes

# WOMEN EARN LESS THAN MEN IN THE SAME JOB CATEGORY

men's earnings  women's earnings  women in each job category

Women's earnings as a percentage of men's earnings, selected job categories, USA, 1981

Percentage of women workers in each job category, USA, 1981

| 64.7 / 100 | 71.8 / 100 | 60.8 / 100 | 52.0 / 100 | 67.0 / 100 | 66.5 / 100 |
|---|---|---|---|---|---|
| 39.5 | 42.8 | 28.4 | 33.0 | 78.4 | 5.6 |
| all occupations | professional and technical | managers and administrators | sales workers | clerical workers | craft workers |

PART TIME WORKERS

Proportion of all women and men at work who work part-time, where data is known, most recent year since 1980, *percentages*

women
men

**Denmark** 47 / 6

**Norway** 45 / <1

**Sweden** 44 / 5

**UK** 44 / 3

**Switzerland** 36 / 5

**Australia** 35 / 5

**Ireland** 33 / 2

**USA** 33 / 18

**West Germany** 29 / 2

**New Zealand** 26 / 5

**Canada** 24 / 6

**Netherlands** 19 / 10

**Austria** 18 / 2

**France** 17 / 2

**Portugal** 17 / 2

**Belgium** 16 / 1

**Finland** 12 / 3

**Italy** 10 / 3

Copyright © Pluto Press

Women are ghettoized in low-paying jobs (see 18. *Job Ghettos*), are often denied promotions, and commonly face outright wage discrimination. They have little job protection (see 20. *Job Protection*), and form the bulk of part-time workers. As a result, women everywhere earn less than men. This is true even when they do the same work as men, and true even in occupations where women form the majority of workers (such as clerical work).

The earnings gap is universal and growing – in spite of equal pay laws which exist in a great number of countries. Such laws are not often enforced, nor do they generally apply to part-time workers or workers in the informal sector, where women predominate. Wage legislation by itself does not remove the inequalities that create the gap in the first place.

Women's relative underpayment in work is a major factor in the growing feminization of poverty.

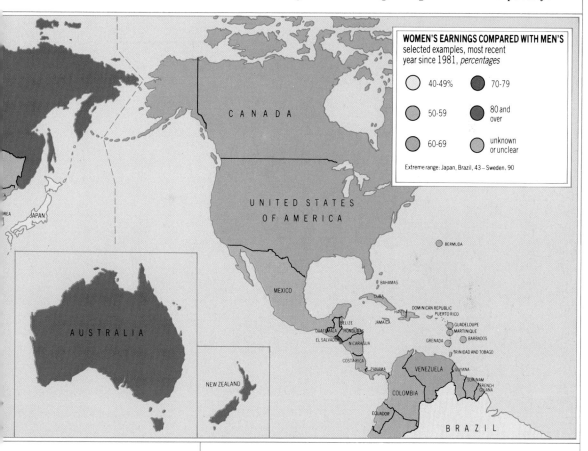

**WOMEN'S EARNINGS COMPARED WITH MEN'S**
selected examples, most recent year since 1981, *percentages*

- 40-49%
- 50-59
- 60-69
- 70-79
- 80 and over
- unknown or unclear

Extreme range: Japan, Brazil, 43 – Sweden, 90

## SOME WOMEN EARN EVEN LESS

Women's earnings as a percentage of white men's earnings, early 1980s

**USA**

- white women: 66
- black women: 60
- Hispanic women: 55
- white men: 100

Black women's earnings as a percentage of white and black men's earnings, early 1980s

**South Africa**

- black women: 8
- white men: 100
- black women: 50
- black men: 100

## IN THE EYES OF THE LAW

National laws and international conventions of equal pay, 1985

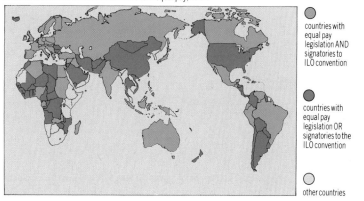

- countries with equal pay legislation AND signatories to ILO convention
- countries with equal pay legislation OR signatories to the ILO convention
- other countries

Sources in Notes

## TAKING THE STRAIN

Women's share of the increase in unemployment 1976-80, selected rich countries, *percentages*

| 100 | 100 | 74.9 | 66.2 | 51.9 | 47.9 | 47.4 | 46.8 | 38.4 | 37.7 |
|-----|-----|------|------|------|------|------|------|------|------|
| Denmark | Finland | Belgium | Italy | UK | Australia | Sweden | Canada | Spain | Japan |

## A WORKER'S RIGHT TO MOTHERHOOD: A MOTHER'S RIGHT TO WORK

States with national legislation providing for maternity leave and pay, 1980s

- maternity leave of 12 weeks or more on full pay (ILO standard)
- maternity leave of 12 weeks or more without full pay
- maternity leave of less than 12 weeks but with full pay
- some leave and pay provisions, but below ILO standard
- no provision, unknown or unclear
- ✔ job tenure a legal provision for pregnant workers

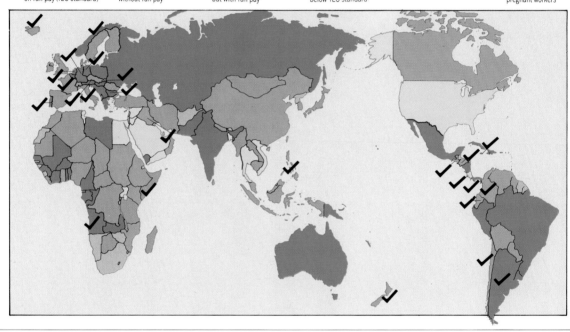

## UNREPRESENTATIVES

Women as a proportion of trade union officials, selected countries, selected examples,1980s, *percentages*

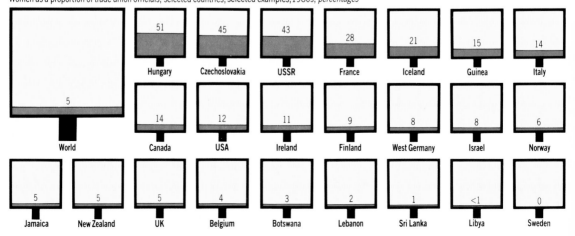

| World | Hungary | Czechoslovakia | USSR | France | Iceland | Guinea | Italy |
|-------|---------|----------------|------|--------|---------|--------|-------|
| 5 | 51 | 45 | 43 | 28 | 21 | 15 | 14 |

| | Canada | USA | Ireland | Finland | West Germany | Israel | Norway |
|--|--------|-----|---------|---------|--------------|--------|--------|
| | 14 | 12 | 11 | 9 | 8 | 8 | 6 |

| Jamaica | New Zealand | UK | Belgium | Botswana | Lebanon | Sri Lanka | Libya | Sweden |
|---------|-------------|-----|---------|----------|---------|-----------|-------|--------|
| 5 | 5 | 5 | 4 | 3 | 2 | 1 | <1 | 0 |

Copyright © Pluto Press

As more women become employed in the formal economy, more of them also become unemployed – at a rate that is rising faster then the rate for men. Women's unemployment is considered to be a less serious problem than men's, but in many countries recent increases in unemployment have been borne almost entirely by women. It is not unusual to find that women's share of registered unemployment is greater than their share of employment.

Many women lose their jobs in trying to balance the conflicting demands that come from having to be both mothers and waged workers. While expected to perform both roles fully and effectively, women receive little support to do so. Maternity policies in most countries leave women with no job protection. And ´unions generally do not take up issues of women's rights, partly because there are few women in policy-making positions within them.

## WOMEN'S SHARE OF UNEMPLOYMENT AND EMPLOYMENT COMPARED

Rich countries, most recent year since 1982

- share of unemployment greater than share of employment
- share of unemployment more or less equal to share of employment
- share of unemployment less than share of employment

Extremes: Portugal, share of unemployment 30 percentage points more than share of employment – UK, share of unemployment 12 percentage points less than share of employment.

Sources in Notes

# INHERITANCE RIGHTS

Countries where women (or some women, living under customary or religious laws) do not have the same rights as men to inherit wealth or property, where known, 1980s

● women do not have the same rights as men   ○ unknown, unclear and others

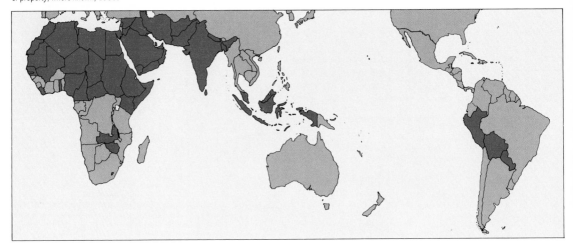

# HOME RULE

Countries where the choice of domicile for a married couple is the husband's by law, and the wife is obliged to follow, where known, 1980s

● women do not have the same rights as men   ○ unknown, unclear and others

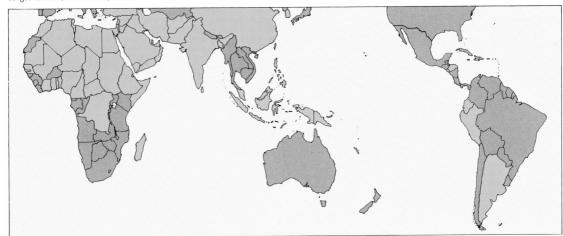

# MANAGING MONEY

Women in finance, insurance and real estate, where known, 1980s, *percentages*

women as a proportion of all workers

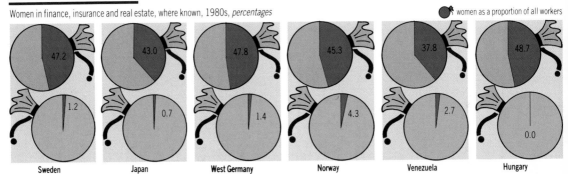

| Sweden | Japan | West Germany | Norway | Venezuela | Hungary |
|--------|-------|--------------|--------|-----------|---------|
| 47.2 | 43.0 | 47.8 | 45.3 | 37.8 | 48.7 |
| 1.2 | 0.7 | 1.4 | 4.3 | 2.7 | 0.0 |

Copyright © Pluto Press

In much of the world, property is the key to survival and women do not have the same rights to property as men. Where women do not share equal rights in marriage, they do not have equal access to property. Where property is held jointly it is almost everywhere controlled by the husband. And amongst the many without property in the world, women are the most destitute.

The ownership of land is a particularly important case. In many countries women are not permitted to own land in their own right, or to control land-use rights without the permission of a male relative. In others where, by custom or practice, they do control land or land-use, land reform is undermining their position because it introduces formal entitlements which almost invariably go to men. Land reform, an important part of many development schemes, benefits women least. Worldwide, women are losing land rights.

In many countries, women cannot inherit either property or wealth, or cannot do so on equal terms with men. In the Islamic code, a daughter's inheritance is limited to one-half of the son's share. In other countries, women are not entitled to an equal share of resources accumulated during marriage.

Women are also denied one of the most basic rights, to choose their domicile. In many countries, it is still a man's prerogative to choose where the family will live. This is usually the right of husband or father, but in some countries it may even pass to a son or a brother.

Even in countries where women are free to own productive assets, they have little and control less. In mining, manufacturing and transport, women are very nearly invisible in the upper reaches of authority. Even in the service industries, normally a more welcoming environment for women, the most important areas, like financial dealings and transactions in landed property, are almost always entirely male preserves.

## LAND RIGHTS

Countries where women (or some women, living under customary or religious laws) do not have the same rights as men to own and administer their own land, or to control and administer communal, tribal or joint landed property, where known, 1980s

● women do not have same rights as men    ● unknown, unclear and others

women as a percentage of administrative and managerial workers

| Panama | Barbados | S. Korea | Portugal | Sri Lanka | Indonesia |
|--------|----------|----------|----------|-----------|-----------|
| 39.8 / 9.3 | 51.4 / 8.3 | 34.6 / 0.0 | 36.6 / 0.0 | 20.4 / 0.0 | 16.9 / 0.0 |

## BOTTOM OF THE CLASS

Copyright © Pluto Press

Countries in which girls form 35 per cent or less of all pupils in secondary schools, 1980s, where known, *percentages*

● boys
● girls

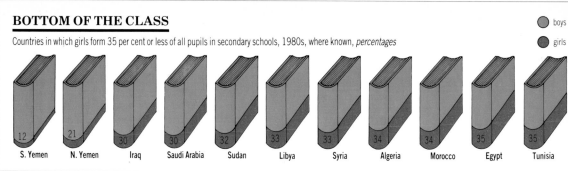

| S. Yemen | N. Yemen | Iraq | Saudi Arabia | Sudan | Libya | Syria | Algeria | Morocco | Egypt | Tunisia |
| 12 | 21 | 30 | 30 | 32 | 33 | 33 | 34 | 34 | 35 | 35 |

## THE BIG LEAP

Relative increase in girls' enrolment over boys' enrolment, primary and secondary schools, 1960–80, 25 countries, *percentages*

740 **Nepal**

644 **Saudi Arabia**

550 **Papua New Guinea**

364 **Chad**

Education is one of the greatest forces for change for women. A woman who can read, write and add numbers has a better chance in life.

In the past twenty-five years, tremendous strides have been made in primary school enrolment; in many countries formal education is no longer seen as wasted on girls.

But the female–male gap still exists at secondary level: in 76 poor countries, less than half of eligible girls are enrolled in secondary school. Where school slots are scarce, boys must compete – but girls are not even expected to try.

Where girls do go to school, they drop out more than boys do. Especially in poor, rural settings, girls are needed at home for chores, or parents do not want their adolescent daughters to mingle with boys. The educational investment is thought to be better spent on sons.

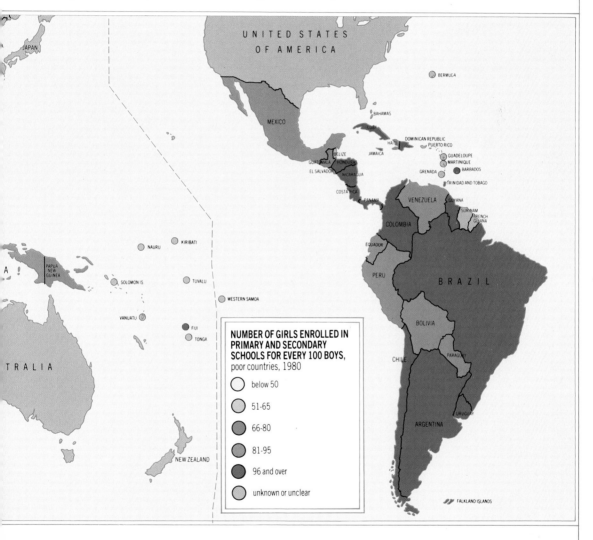

**NUMBER OF GIRLS ENROLLED IN PRIMARY AND SECONDARY SCHOOLS FOR EVERY 100 BOYS,** poor countries, 1980

- below 50
- 51-65
- 66-80
- 81-95
- 96 and over
- unknown or unclear

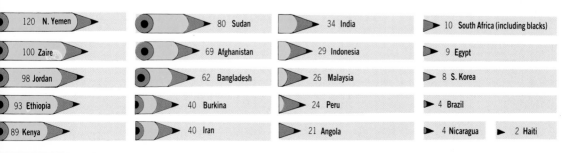

| | | | |
|---|---|---|---|
| 120 N. Yemen | 80 Sudan | 34 India | 10 South Africa (including blacks) |
| 100 Zaire | 69 Afghanistan | 29 Indonesia | 9 Egypt |
| 98 Jordan | 62 Bangladesh | 26 Malaysia | 8 S. Korea |
| 93 Ethiopia | 40 Burkina | 24 Peru | 4 Brazil |
| 89 Kenya | 40 Iran | 21 Angola | 4 Nicaragua | 2 Haiti |

# BY DEGREES

Year of women's admission to some famous universities

opening year ◆   year women admitted ◇

| | 1100 | 1500 | 1900 |
|---|---|---|---|
| London | | | 1836 ◆ / 1878 ◇ |
| Cambridge | 1284 ◆ | | 1873 ◇ |
| Oxford | 1167 ◆ | | 1878 ◇ |
| Dublin | | 1592 ◆ | 1904 ◇ |
| Harvard | | 1636 ◆ | 1894 ◇ |

| | 1100 | 1500 | 1900 |
|---|---|---|---|
| Yale | | 1701 ◆ | 1969 ◇ |
| Columbia | | 1754 ◆ | 1889 ◇ |
| Toronto | | 1827 ◆ | 1884 ◇ |
| McGill | | 1821 ◆ | 1884 ◇ |
| Oslo | | 1811 ◆ | 1882 ◇ |

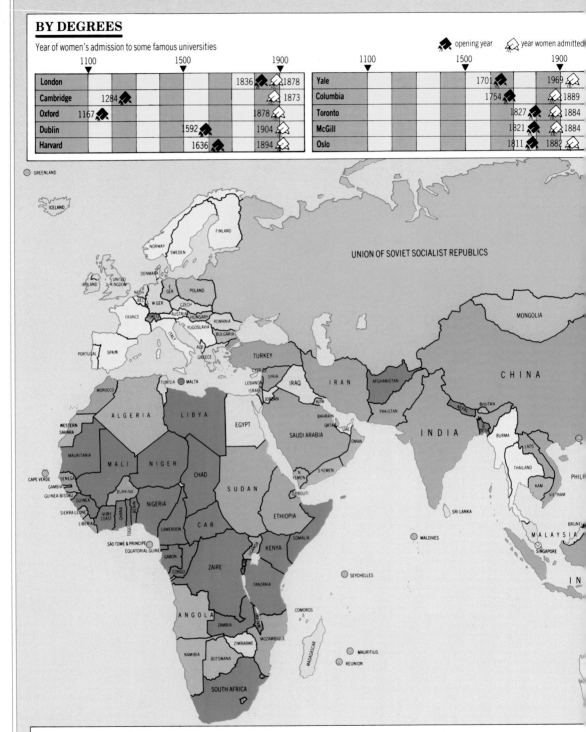

# GENDER OF STUDIES

Degrees conferred on women, by field of study, USA, 1980, *percentages*

BA degree *italic*   PhD **bold**

| field | BA | PhD |
|---|---|---|
| engineering | *9* | **4** |
| physical sciences | *24* | **13** |
| philosophy | *27* | **24** |
| computer science | *30* | **11** |

| field | BA | PhD |
|---|---|---|
| geography | *32* | **14** |
| business/management | *37* | **15** |
| mathematics | *42* | **14** |
| social sciences | *44* | **27** |

| field | BA | PhD |
|---|---|---|
| fine & applied arts | *63* | **37** |
| education | *74* | **44** |
| social work | *81* | **50** |
| library science | *95* | **56** |

Professional degrees conferred on women, USA, 1980, *percentages*

| | |
|---|---|
| dentistry | 13 |
| theology | 17 |
| medicine | 23 |
| law | 30 |

Copyright © Pluto Press

For women to perform effectively in a world of professionals, they need access to higher education. While girls have made great progress in school enrolment, almost nowhere do women match men on the university campus. This is true despite dramatic enrolment increases in some countries.

Often, women cannot afford to go to university, do not believe in their own abilities, and are not encouraged to succeed academically. Where women do attend, they are often encouraged into female disciplinary ghettos such as social work, education and library science. This is now beginning to change, however, as more and more women turn to the sciences and enter the professions.

The oldest and most famous universities long excluded women. It is only recently, since the wave of women's liberation at the turn of the century, that women have appeared on campus at all.

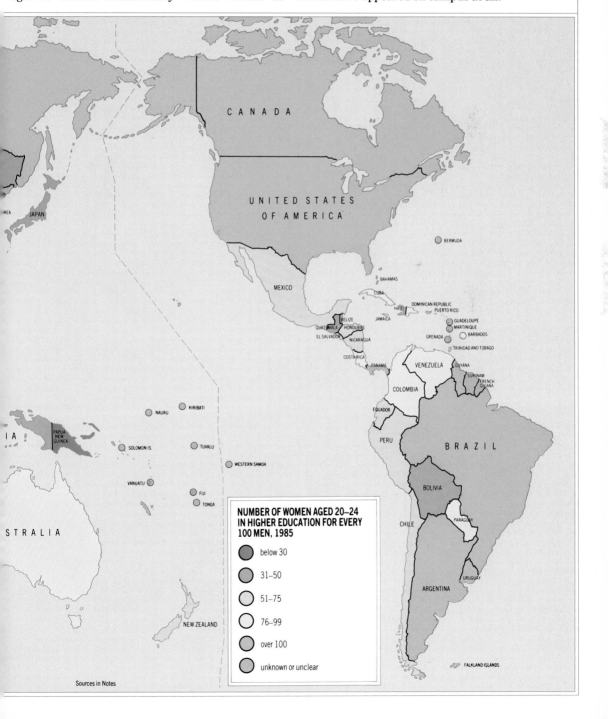

**NUMBER OF WOMEN AGED 20–24 IN HIGHER EDUCATION FOR EVERY 100 MEN, 1985**

- below 30
- 31–50
- 51–75
- 76–99
- over 100
- unknown or unclear

Sources in Notes

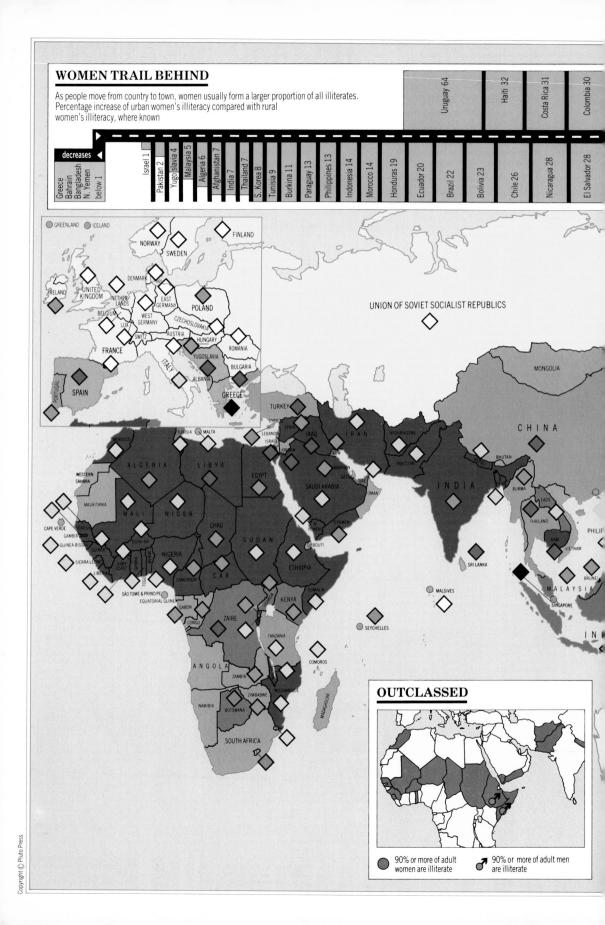

# WOMEN TRAIL BEHIND

As people move from country to town, women usually form a larger proportion of all illiterates. Percentage increase of urban women's illiteracy compared with rural women's illiteracy, where known

decreases ◄

Greece
Bahrain
Bangladesh
N. Yemen
below 1

Israel 1
Pakistan 2
Yugoslavia 4
Malaysia 5
Algeria 6
Afghanistan 7
India 7
Thailand 7
S. Korea 8
Tunisia 9
Burkina 11
Paraguay 13
Philippines 13
Indonesia 14
Morocco 14
Honduras 19
Ecuador 20
Brazil 22
Bolivia 23
Chile 26
Nicaragua 28
El Salvador 28

Uruguay 64
Haiti 32
Costa Rica 31
Colombia 30

UNION OF SOVIET SOCIALIST REPUBLICS

## OUTCLASSED

● 90% or more of adult women are illiterate

➤ 90% or more of adult men are illiterate

Copyright © Pluto Press

Adults who can neither read nor write also cannot participate fully in modern life. More adult women than men fall into this category: two-thirds of the world's illiterates are women; in seventeen countries over 90 per cent of women are illiterate.

This is largely the legacy of women's relative confinement to domestic and private life, and the widespread prejudice against educating girls.

Almost everywhere the gap in literacy between women and men is widening. This is especially true in cities, where men have more opportunities – often at work – to learn to read and write. So, while literacy for both women and men is higher in cities than in rural areas, urbanization more often than not leaves women at a relative disadvantage. Women's illiteracy is also more hidden than men's, and official figures are known to underestimate the problem.

**ILLITERATE WOMEN AS A PROPORTION OF ALL ADULT WOMEN**
most recent year since 1970, *percentages*

- over 75
- 50-75
- 25-49
- 10-24
- below 10
- unknown or unclear

**WOMEN'S ILLITERACY COMPARED WITH MEN'S**

- women's illiteracy more than 200% higher than men's
- 101-200% higher
- 51-100% higher
- up to 50% higher
- more or less equal
- men's illiteracy higher than women's

## ON TAP

Proportion of population with
safe drinking water, poor
countries, 1980, *percentages*

- ⬤ below 25
- ⬤ 26-50
- ⬤ 51-75
- ⬤ over 75
- ⬤ unknown or unclear

## POISONED WELLS

People (predominantly women)
affected by some major
illnesses acquired while
drawing water, *millions*

malaria 300
river blindness 20-30
elephantiasis 270

## ANAEMIA

Women who are anaemic, 1975, *millions*

ASIA excluding China 296.4

AFRICA 92.2

LATIN AMERICA 74.6

☐ = 1 million

Copyright © Pluto Press

The world's women are chronically fatigued, and many are anaemic from malnourishment. This means that when women are exposed to disease they are especially susceptible.

It is women who collect, cook with, and wash family and home using local water. If the water source is far away, unclean, or in short supply, it is primarily women who suffer from the resulting fatigue and disease. And it is women who are held responsible for the poor health of their families when polluted water and inadequate sanitation make the practice of good hygiene either difficult or well-nigh impossible.

Women sow, reap, harvest and cook the world's food, but serve themselves last and least. When food is scarce, women suffer most and future generations are handicapped from birth by malnourished pregnant and nursing mothers.

**PROPORTION OF INFANTS WITH LOW BIRTH-WEIGHTS**
1979, *percentages*

- above 30
- 20.1-30
- 15.1-20
- 8.1-15
- 8 and below
- unknown or unclear

♀ percentage of pregnant women who are anaemic, most recent year

Sources in Notes

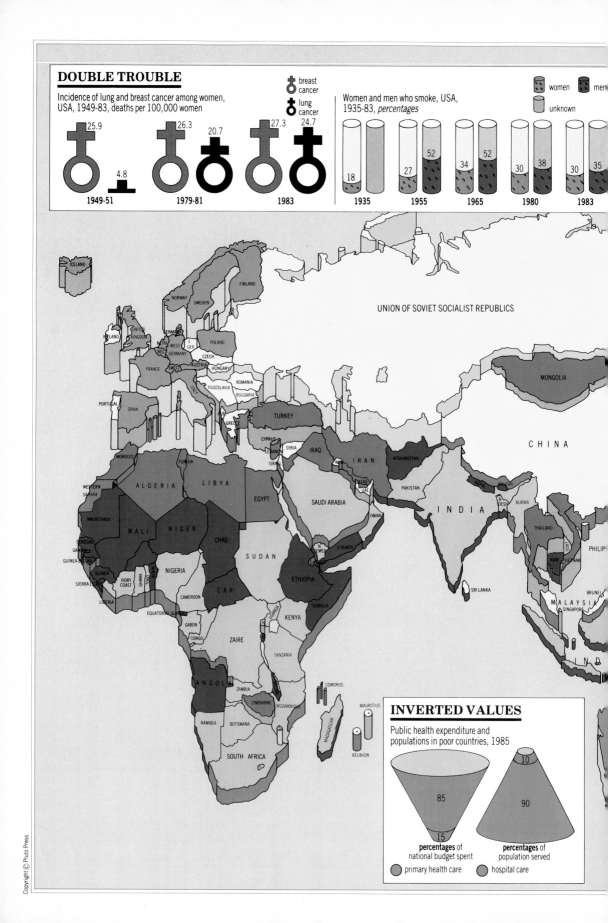

# DOUBLE TROUBLE

Incidence of lung and breast cancer among women, USA, 1949-83, deaths per 100,000 women

♀ breast cancer
♂ lung cancer

25.9
4.8
**1949-51**

26.3
20.7
**1979-81**

27.3
24.7
**1983**

Women and men who smoke, USA, 1935-83, *percentages*

women | men
unknown

18 | | **1935**
27 | 52 | **1955**
34 | 52 | **1965**
30 | 38 | **1980**
30 | 35 | **1983**

UNION OF SOVIET SOCIALIST REPUBLICS

CHINA

MONGOLIA

INDIA

## INVERTED VALUES

Public health expenditure and populations in poor countries, 1985

85
15
**percentages** of national budget spent

10
90
**percentages** of population served

⬤ primary health care
⬤ hospital care

Copyright © Pluto Press

Women are biologically stronger than men. But where girls' and women's health is neglected, that edge is lost. In poor countries and in rural settings, constant childbearing, lack of village-level health care, and the neglect of infant girls in favour of boys, all make living more hazardous for women.

Working harder and longer, eating less and worse, earning less and having little control over resources – all while giving birth and nursing – make women more vulnerable to disease. This is particularly true in poor countries, where death from infectious and parasitic disease is prevalent.

In the rich world, where women live long enough to develop degenerative and environmental diseases, they are increasingly taking the same chances as men – smoking, drinking and taking drugs – and are increasingly in danger from cancer, heart disease and strokes.

**WOMEN'S LIFE EXPECTANCY AT BIRTH**
1980

- below 45
- 55.1-65
- over 75
- 45.1-55
- 65.1-75
- unknown or unclear

**WOMEN LIVE LONGER THAN MEN**
Difference in years, 1980

- above 6
- 4.1-6
- 3.1-4
- 3 and below

It is war, famine, drought, and oppression that turn people into international refugees. There are now over 15 million refugees in the world; the large majority are women and their dependent children.

Refugees often escape from one state of misery only to enter another of equal, if not greater misery. Countries of asylum are often as poor as the countries they flee. Women often flee from one country where their status is low, to another where it is no better; as refugees, they sink even lower. Refugee women are among the poorest of the world's poor, and they have little control over their fate: women generally have no say in the administration of refugee camps, or in the development of national and international refugee policies.

With no protection of family or state, women refugees are under constant threats – of which rape is the most generally pervasive.

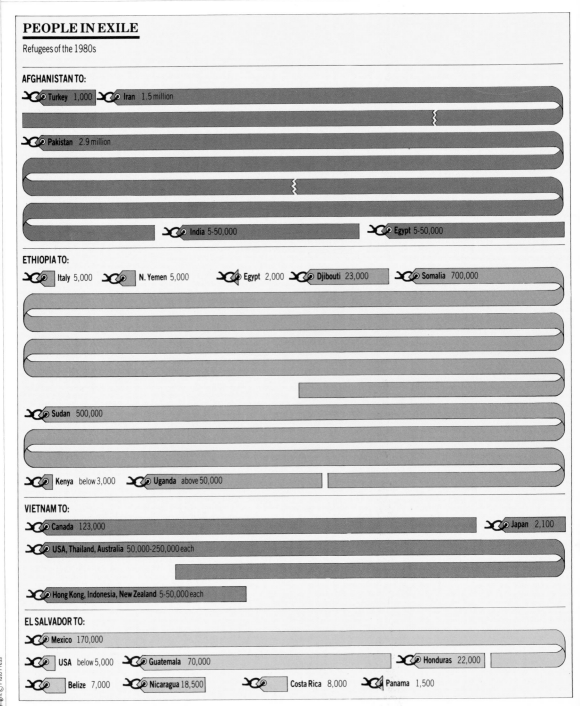

**PEOPLE IN EXILE**

Refugees of the 1980s

**AFGHANISTAN TO:**
Turkey 1,000   Iran 1.5 million
Pakistan 2.9 million
India 5-50,000   Egypt 5-50,000

**ETHIOPIA TO:**
Italy 5,000   N. Yemen 5,000   Egypt 2,000   Djibouti 23,000   Somalia 700,000
Sudan 500,000
Kenya below 3,000   Uganda above 50,000

**VIETNAM TO:**
Canada 123,000   Japan 2,100
USA, Thailand, Australia 50,000-250,000 each
Hong Kong, Indonesia, New Zealand 5-50,000 each

**EL SALVADOR TO:**
Mexico 170,000
USA below 5,000   Guatemala 70,000   Honduras 22,000
Belize 7,000   Nicaragua 18,500   Costa Rica 8,000   Panama 1,500

Copyright © Pluto Press

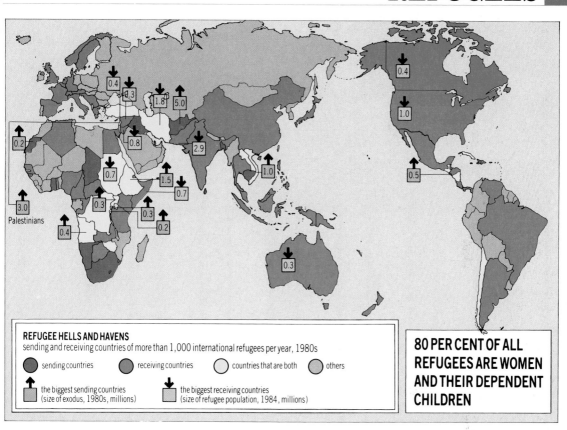

## REFUGEE HELLS AND HAVENS
sending and receiving countries of more than 1,000 international refugees per year, 1980s

● sending countries    ● receiving countries    ○ countries that are both    ○ others

↑ the biggest sending countries (size of exodus, 1980s, millions)

↓ the biggest receiving countries (size of refugee population, 1984, millions)

## 80 PER CENT OF ALL REFUGEES ARE WOMEN AND THEIR DEPENDENT CHILDREN

## THE PALESTINIAN EXILES
The number of Palestinian refugees in the 1980s

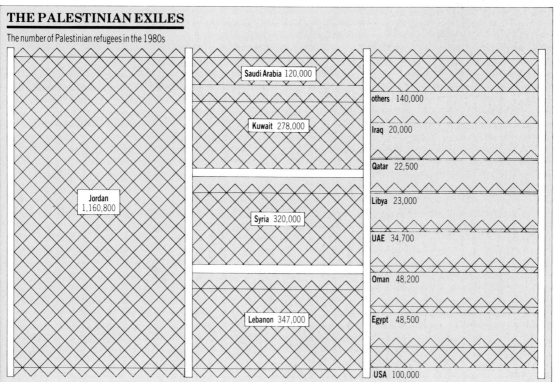

Jordan 1,160,800

Saudi Arabia 120,000

Kuwait 278,000

Syria 320,000

Lebanon 347,000

others 140,000

Iraq 20,000

Qatar 22,500

Libya 23,000

UAE 34,700

Oman 48,200

Egypt 48,500

USA 100,000

## ALL IN THE FAMILY

Single-parent families headed by women as a proportion of all families, USA, 1984, *percentages*

| | |
| --- | --- |
| 16 | all |
| 12 | whites |
| 42 | blacks |
| 22 | Hispanics |

## POOR FAMILIES

Proportion of families categorized as poor by the government, USA, 1981, *percentages*

| | all | white | black | Hispanic |
| --- | --- | --- | --- | --- |
| single-parent families headed by women | 35 | 27 | 53 | 53 |
| single-parent families headed by men | 10 | 9 | 19 | 19 |
| husband-wife families | 7 | 6 | 15 | 15 |

## LIVING LONGER

Proportions of women and men over aged 60, selected examples, 1985, *percentages*

women   men

| | women | men |
| --- | --- | --- |
| Australia | 13 | 16 |
| Austria | 15 | 24 |
| El Salvador | 5 | 6 |
| Finland | 13 | 21 |
| France | 15 | 20 |
| India | 6 | 6 |
| Indonesia | 5 | 6 |
| Japan | 12 | 16 |
| Kenya | 3 | 3 |
| Poland | 11 | 16 |
| Singapore | 7 | 8 |
| Sweden | 21 | 25 |
| Switzerland | 17 | 27 |
| Syria | 4 | 5 |
| UK | 17 | 23 |
| USA | 14 | 18 |

Copyright © Pluto Press

Women everywhere control fewer resources and reap a lesser share of the world's wealth than men; it follows from this that when women have to support families and themselves on their own, they end up poorer than men.

In the USA, 78 per cent of all people living in poverty are women or children under 18 years old. Statistics from all over the world tell the same story: no matter how poverty is measured, the poor population is largely and increasingly comprised of women and their dependent children. This is what is known as the feminization of poverty.

Worldwide, one-third of all households are now headed by women. Women outlive men and commonly spend some of their older years alone.

The poverty that is disproportionately borne by women, is especially borne by those with children and by older women.

## FAMILIES OF WOMEN

Number of households headed by women as a proportion of all households, most recent year since mid-1970s, *percentages*

below 10　　10-20　　21-30　　31 and above

| | | | | | | |
|---|---|---|---|---|---|---|
| Guinea | Iran | Jordan | Netherlands | Niger | Burkina | Italy |
| Argentina | Brazil | Canada | Costa Rica | Cuba | Ecuador | Finland |
| France | Indonesia | South Korea | Liberia | Madagascar | Malaysia | Mali |
| Mexico | Morocco | Poland | Sri Lanka | Syria | Taiwan | Thailand |
| USA | UK | Tunisia | Turkey | Zambia | Belize | El Salvador |
| Ghana | Guyana | Malawi | Mauritania | Rwanda | Sudan | Trinidad & Tobago |
| Venezuela | Barbados | Botswana | Denmark | Dominica | Honduras | Jamaica |
| Kenya | Lesotho | Nicaragua | Panama | Paraguay | Vietnam | Zimbabwe |

Sources in Notes

# WHEN WOMEN WON THE VOTE

■ □ Each dot represents one country

1900 1910 1920 1930 1940 1950 1960 1970 1980

GREENLAND
ICELAND
FINLAND
NORWAY
SWEDEN
DENMARK
UNITED KINGDOM
IRELAND
NETH
BEL
W GER
E GER
POLAND
CZECH
AUSTRIA
HUNGARY
ROMANIA
YUGOSLAVIA
BULGARIA
FRANCE
ITALY
PORTUGAL SPAIN
GREECE
TUNISIA MALTA
MOROCCO
CYPRUS
LEBANON SYRIA
ISRAEL
JORDAN
IRAQ
IRAN
AFGHANISTAN
PAKISTAN

UNION OF SOVIET SOCIALIST REPUBLICS

MONGOLIA

CHINA

TURKEY

WESTERN SAHARA
ALGERIA LIBYA EGYPT
MAURITANIA
MALI NIGER CHAD
CAPE VERDE
SENEGAL
GAMBIA
GUINEA-BISSAU GUINEA
SIERRA LEONE
LIBERIA
BURKINA
IVORY COAST GHANA
TOGO
BENIN
NIGERIA
CAMEROON
SUDAN
CAR
ETHIOPIA
SÃO TOME & PRINCIPE
EQUATORIAL GUINEA
GABON
CONGO
ZAIRE
UGANDA
KENYA
SOMALIA
RWANDA
BURUNDI
TANZANIA

BAHRAIN
QATAR UAE
SAUDI ARABIA
OMAN
N YEMEN
S YEMEN
DJIBOUTI

NEPAL
BHUTAN
BANGLADESH
INDIA
BURMA
LAOS
THAILAND
KAM
VIETNAM
PHIL
SRI LANKA
MALDIVES
BRUNEI
MALAYSIA
SINGAPORE
IN

SEYCHELLES

ANGOLA
ZAMBIA
ZIMBABWE
MOZAMBIQUE
NAMIBIA BOTSWANA
COMOROS
MADAGASCAR
MAURITIUS
REUNION

SOUTH AFRICA

## VOTING LESS OFTEN...

Difference between the proportions of women and men who
intended to vote in national elections, early 1980s *percentages*

| West Germany | 13.1 | Netherlands | 6.9 |
| Ireland | 11.7 | Italy | 6.7 |
| Denmark | 8.0 | UK | 2.7 |
| Greece | 7.2 | France | 2.6 |

## BUT CLOSING THE GAP

Difference between the proportions of women and men who voted
in US presidential elections, *percentages*

● women ● men

| 7.3 | 5.7 | 3.4 | 1.4 | 0.3 | 0 |
| 1964 | 1968 | 1972 | 1976 | 1980 | 1984 |

Copyright © Pluto Press

The right to vote is an important measure of full citizenship, and an important means for women to gain other rights.

Voting rights for women were often strongly resisted almost everywhere, and men gained the vote before women; in a few countries this is still so. In some countries, white women or women with property or education had the vote before others. In many, women won the vote as part of a larger social reordering, such as the transfer from colonial to national rule. For many women, then, voting is a recent privilege.

Worldwide, women tend to vote less than men, but the gap is narrowing.

Since women everywhere are a slight majority of the population, if women voted in equal proportion to men they would actually represent an electoral majority.

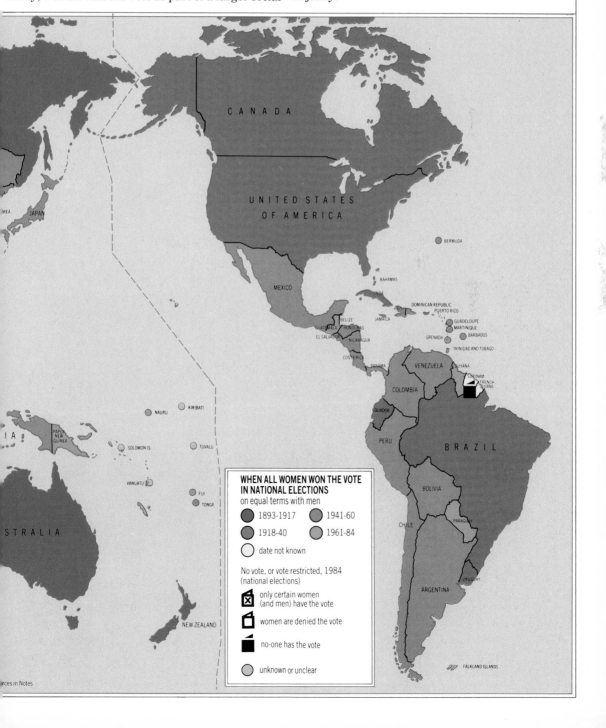

**WHEN ALL WOMEN WON THE VOTE IN NATIONAL ELECTIONS**
on equal terms with men

- 1893-1917
- 1918-40
- 1941-60
- 1961-84
- date not known

No vote, or vote restricted, 1984 (national elections)

- ☒ only certain women (and men) have the vote
- ☐ women are denied the vote
- ■ no-one has the vote
- ○ unknown or unclear

Sources in Notes

Most governments are governments of men. No-where do women hold more than a minority of seats in national legislatures. In many of the countries where they appear to have a greater voice, the legislatures they serve are in fact powerless or symbolic. There are only a handful of countries in which women have significant representation in a significant legislature. In Scandinavia, women have the best – and the earliest – record of representation in government.

That women have the right to participate in government does not mean they exercise much power in most countries. The gender gap in govern-ment is greatest at the top of the hierarchy. The powerful and prestigious government posts are typically held by men across the entire spectrum of political systems. Women in cabinet-level positions remain exceptions to the rule everywhere.

## THE GATES OPEN SLOWLY

Date of women's first entry into high-level political positions compared with date of first suffrage, selected examples

date of first suffrage    first woman to cabinet post

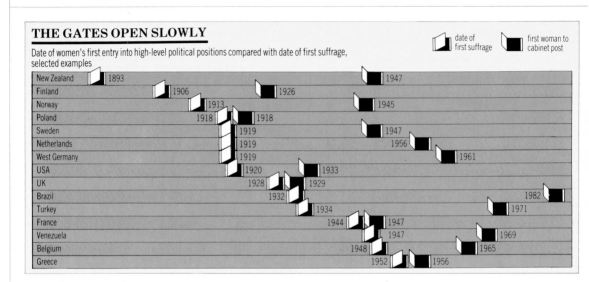

## EARLY MOMENTUM

Early growth of women's representation in national legislatures, Scandinavia *percentages*

Copyright © Pluto Press

Sources in Notes

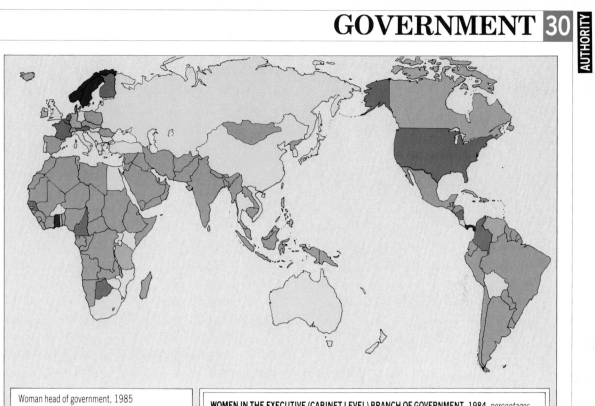

Woman head of government, 1985

 Iceland, United Kingdom, Yugoslavia, Dominica

**WOMEN IN THE EXECUTIVE (CABINET LEVEL) BRANCH OF GOVERNMENT, 1984** *percentages*

● above 20    ● 11-20    ● 6-10    ○ 5 and below    unknown or unclear

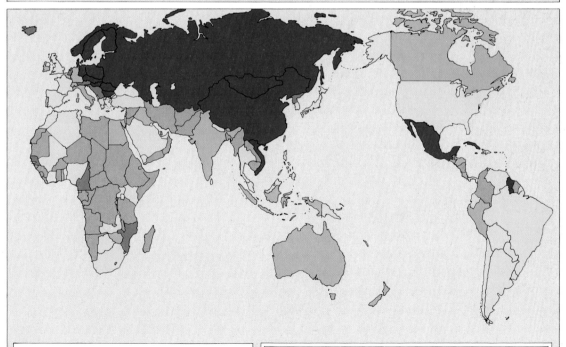

Significant representation in significant legislature

 Denmark, Norway, Sweden, Finland

**WOMEN IN THE LEGISLATIVE BRANCH OF GOVERNMENT, 1984** *percentages*

 ● above 20    ● 11-20    ● 6-10    ○ 5 and below    unknown or unclear

Sources in Notes

# THE CRIMINAL ELEMENTS

Women and men compared, UK, USA and Sweden, early 1980s, *percentages*

● women  ● men

### Prison sentences, UK, 1982

| burglary | robbery | theft, fraud and forgery | violence against the person |
|---|---|---|---|
| 99 | 98 | 95 | 98 |
| 1 | 2 | 5 | 2 |

### Arrests, USA, 1983

| murder | robbery | arson | aggravated assault | larceny and theft |
|---|---|---|---|---|
| 87 | 93 | 89 | 87 | 71 |
| 13 | 7 | 11 | 13 | 29 |

### Convictions, Sweden, 1983

| assault and battery | petty larceny | theft | fraud | drug offences |
|---|---|---|---|---|
| 94 | 61 | 89 | 76 | 85 |
| 6 | 39 | 11 | 24 | 15 |

# BARRED WOMEN

Women as a proportion of all lawyers, where data is known, early 1980s, *percentages*

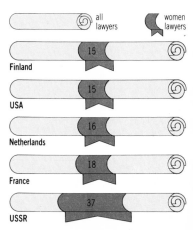

all lawyers
women lawyers

**Women are banned from studying law in Iran and Saudi Arabia**

| | |
|---|---|
| Thailand | 2 |
| Japan | 3 |
| India | 3 |
| Kenya | <5 |
| Syria | <5 |
| Spain | 6 |
| Italy | 10 |
| Portugal | 12 |
| Bulgaria | 15 |
| Finland | 15 |
| USA | 15 |
| Netherlands | 16 |
| France | 18 |
| USSR | 37 |

Copyright © Pluto Press

There are wide differences in how 'crimes' and 'criminals' are officially defined and reported. But, regardless of definition, most crimes are committed by men, and everywhere, women constitute a very small proportion of all criminals.

In most countries, women's crime rates are now increasing rapidly and at a much faster rate than men's. But women's share of total crimes remains minor.

The gap between women and men is greatest in violent crimes. Typically, more than 90 per cent of incidents involving violence are committed by men. Theft and larceny are the crimes most commonly attributed to women.

Women have very little representation in the administration of law. They are banned from studying law in two countries, but in general they are a small and growing proportion of all lawyers.

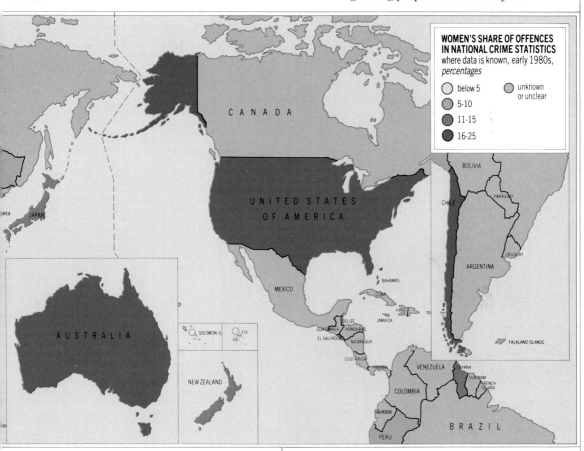

**WOMEN'S SHARE OF OFFENCES IN NATIONAL CRIME STATISTICS**
where data is known, early 1980s, *percentages*

- below 5
- 5-10
- 11-15
- 16-25
- unknown or unclear

## ARRESTING WOMEN

Percentage increase in the number of arrests of women and men, 1969-78, USA, *percentages*

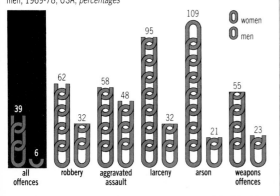

- women
- men

| | all offences | robbery | aggravated assault | larceny | arson | weapons offences |
|---|---|---|---|---|---|---|
| women | 39 | 62 | 58 | 95 | 109 | 55 |
| men | 6 | 32 | 48 | 32 | 21 | 23 |

## WOMEN IN TROUBLE

**UK**
crimes of women prisoners, 1982, *percentages*

- 27 crimes against property
- 17 crimes against persons
- 56 other

**Sweden**
crimes of convicted women, 1983, *percentages*

- 36 crimes against property
- 3 motoring offences
- 19 crimes against persons
- 42 other

**India**
crimes of women arrested, 1975, *percentages*

- 51 theft
- 8 riot
- 19 crimes against persons
- 22 other

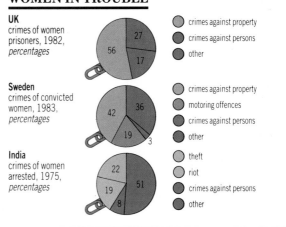

Sources in Notes

# WOMEN FIGHTERS

Countries where women have been combatants in revolutionary armies and civil wars, where known, 1975-85

| Nicaragua | Guatemala | El Salvador | Ethiopia | Guinea-Bissau | Mozambique | Angola | Namibia | Iran | Philippines | Vietnam | Zimbabwe |

except for medical corps

university women only

except for medical corps

GREENLAND
ICELAND
IRELAND
UNITED KINGDOM
NETH
BEL
W GER
FRANCE
PORTUGAL
SPAIN
NORWAY
SWEDEN
DENMARK
E GER
POLAND
CZECH
AUSTRIA
HUNGARY
YUGOSLAVIA
ITALY
ALB
GREECE
ROMANIA
BULGARIA
FINLAND
UNION OF SOVIET SOCIALIST REPUBLICS
MONGOLIA
CHINA
TURKEY
CYPRUS
SYRIA
LEBANON
ISRAEL
IRAQ
JORDAN
IRAN
AFGHANISTAN
PAKISTAN
INDIA
NEPAL
BHUTAN
B DESH
BURMA
LAOS
THAILAND
KAM
VIETNAM
PH
MALAYSIA
SINGAPORE
BRU
MOROCCO
TUNISIA
MALTA
ALGERIA
LIBYA
EGYPT
KUW
BAHRAIN
QATAR
UAE
SAUDI ARABIA
OMAN
N YEMEN
S YEMEN
WESTERN SAHARA
MAURITANIA
MALI
NIGER
CHAD
SUDAN
DJIBOUTI
ETHIOPIA
SOMALIA
CAPE VERDE
SENEGAL
GAMBIA
GUINEA-BISSAU
GUINEA
SIERRA LEONE
LIBERIA
IVORY COAST
GHANA
BURKINA
TOGO
BENIN
NIGERIA
CAMEROON
CAR
SÃO TOME & PRINCIPE
EQUATORIAL GUINEA
GABON
CONGO
ZAIRE
UGANDA
KENYA
TANZANIA
SRI LANKA
MALDIVES
SEYCHELLES
COMOROS
ANGOLA
ZAMBIA
MALAWI
MOZAMBIQUE
ZIMBABWE
NAMIBIA
BOTSWANA
MADAGASCAR
MAURITIUS
REUNION

# WOMEN IN NATO

Percentage of women in armed forces of NATO countries, 1983

● men ● women  * medical corps officers only

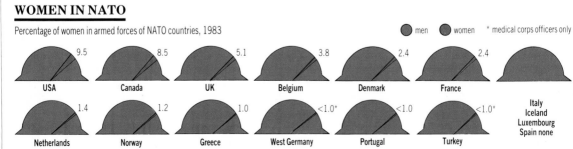

| USA | Canada | UK | Belgium | Denmark | France |
|---|---|---|---|---|---|
| 9.5 | 8.5 | 5.1 | 3.8 | 2.4 | 2.4 |

| Netherlands | Norway | Greece | West Germany | Portugal | Turkey | Italy Iceland Luxembourg Spain none |
|---|---|---|---|---|---|---|
| 1.4 | 1.2 | 1.0 | <1.0* | <1.0 | <1.0* | |

Copyright © Pluto Press

Serving one's country as part of the military is widely held to be an honour and an act of patriotism. Military service also brings economic and social rewards, especially in countries where the armed forces are politically powerful or where they form the government.

Most governments do not want women in their armed forces. But many now feel that they are running short on acceptable male recruits. So an uneasy compromise adopted in many countries is to permit women into the services, but to deny them certain roles. Combat, in particular, is considered unnatural for women, although large numbers of them have fought in civil wars and revolutionary armies.

In wartime, even the regular armies resort to using women in service, but after the war they are expected to return home.

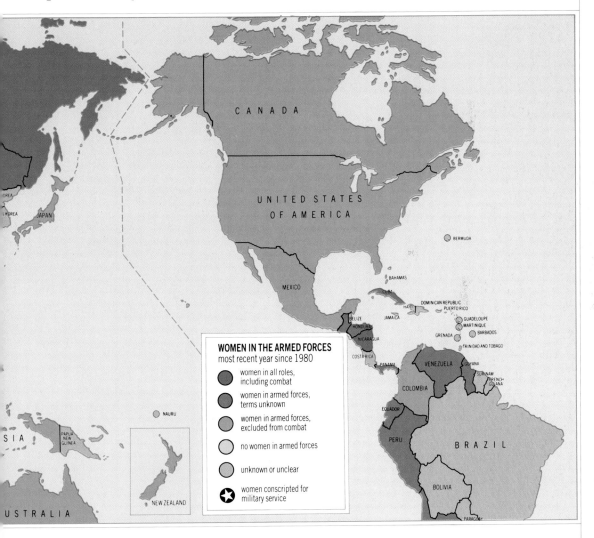

**WOMEN IN THE ARMED FORCES**
most recent year since 1980

- women in all roles, including combat
- women in armed forces, terms unknown
- women in armed forces, excluded from combat
- no women in armed forces
- unknown or unclear
- women conscripted for military service

## WARTIME WARRIORS

Women in the armed forces of the UK, 1939-46

number of women · women as percentage of total

| | | | 386,000 | 420,400 | 445,200 | 453,200 | 449,100 | 450,000 | 436,000 | 415,800 | |
| --- | --- | --- | --- | --- | --- | --- | --- | --- | --- | --- | --- |
| 36,100 | 66,900 | 205,100 | | | | | | | | | 137,400 |
| 2.3 | 2.3 | 5.4 | 8.7 | 9.1 | 9.4 | 9.4 | 9.2 | 9.2 | 8.8 | 8.2 | 6.7 |
| Dec 1939 | Dec 1940 | Dec 1941 | Dec 1942 | Mar 1943 | June 1943 | Sept 1943 | Dec 1943 | Mar 1944 | Dec 1944 | June 1945 | June 1946 |

# WOMEN DO MOST OF THE WORK

Number of women health care workers (nurses and doctors) for every 100 men health care workers
selected examples, most recent year since 1975

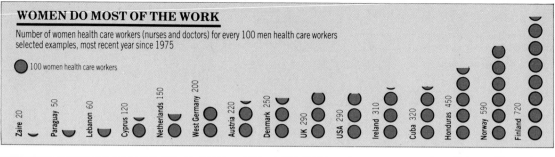

100 women health care workers

Zaire 20 · Paraguay 50 · Lebanon 60 · Cyprus 120 · Netherlands 150 · West Germany 200 · Austria 220 · Denmark 250 · UK 290 · USA 290 · Ireland 310 · Cuba 320 · Honduras 450 · Norway 590 · Finland 720

# BUT WOMEN HAVE LITTLE SAY

where data is known, most recent year since 1975

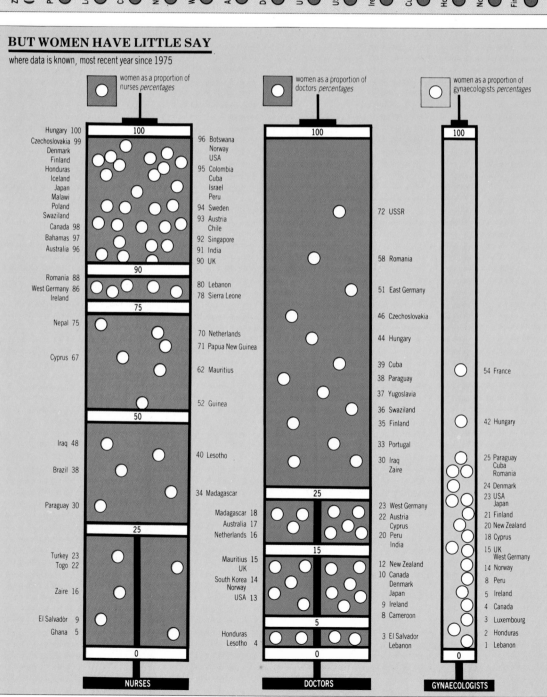

women as a proportion of nurses *percentages*

women as a proportion of doctors *percentages*

women as a proportion of gynaecologists *percentages*

**NURSES**

Hungary 100
Czechoslovakia 99
Denmark
Finland
Honduras
Iceland
Japan
Malawi
Poland
Swaziland
Canada 98
Bahamas 97
Australia 96
96 Botswana / Norway / USA
95 Colombia / Cuba / Israel / Peru
94 Sweden
93 Austria / Chile
92 Singapore
91 India
90 UK

100 — 90

Romania 88
West Germany 86
Ireland
80 Lebanon
78 Sierra Leone

75

Nepal 75
70 Netherlands
71 Papua New Guinea

Cyprus 67
62 Mauritius

52 Guinea

50

Iraq 48
40 Lesotho

Brazil 38

34 Madagascar

Paraguay 30

25

Turkey 23
Togo 22

Zaire 16

El Salvador 9
Ghana 5

0

**DOCTORS**

72 USSR

58 Romania

51 East Germany

46 Czechoslovakia

44 Hungary

39 Cuba
38 Paraguay
37 Yugoslavia
36 Swaziland
35 Finland

33 Portugal

30 Iraq / Zaire

25

Madagascar 18
Australia 17
Netherlands 16
23 West Germany
22 Austria / Cyprus
20 Peru / India

15

Mauritius 15
UK
South Korea 14
Norway
USA 13
12 New Zealand
10 Canada / Denmark / Japan
9 Ireland
8 Cameroon

5

Honduras
Lesotho 4
3 El Salvador / Lebanon

0

**GYNAECOLOGISTS**

54 France

42 Hungary

25 Paraguay / Cuba / Romania
24 Denmark
23 USA / Japan
21 Finland
20 New Zealand
18 Cyprus
15 UK / West Germany
14 Norway
8 Peru
5 Ireland
4 Canada
3 Luxembourg
2 Honduras
1 Lebanon

0

Sources in Notes

Women constitute by far the greater number of health care workers in most countries, but they are not represented evenly throughout the profession. They are concentrated mostly in one sector: nursing, which being 'women's work', is accorded the lowest pay, the least prestige and the least power. So while they do the greater share of health care work, women receive the smaller share of benefits.

The status, pay and power imbalance in health care is shifting slowly as more women become doctors, and as nurses press demands for better recognition of the work they do. But the gap is still large, even in that part of the profession that deals exclusively with women, gynaecology.

The picture is much the same in teaching. Most teachers in the world are women, but most women teachers occupy the bottom rung of the educational ladder.

## PACEMAKERS IN TEACHING

Women as a proportion of teachers at four levels of education selected examples, most recent year since 1975, *percentages*

3rd level (* university only)
2nd level
primary
pre-primary

unknown or unclear

## WOMEN AS A PROPORTION OF ALL TEACHERS

World average

Argentina — 56, 63, 92, 100
Australia — 45, 71, 100
Austria — 16*, 52, 77, 99
Brazil — 21*, 53, 87, 98

Bulgaria — 33*, 54, 75, 100
Canada — 21, 40, 67, 100
China — 25, 27, 37, 82
Colombia — 13*, 45, 79, 93
Congo — 9*, 11, 26, 100
Czechoslovakia — 27*, 47, 80, 100
Ecuador — 7, 37, 66, 96
Egypt — 25*, 31, 48, 90

El Salvador — 23, 27, 67, 88
Finland — 22*, 61, 100
France — 65, 99
West Germany — 18, 41, 62
India — 30, 26, 8
Italy — 58, 87, 100

Japan — 10*, 26, 57, 88
South Korea — 15*, 26, 39, 86
Libya — 4*, 24, 47, 100
Malaysia — 28*, 44, 42, 99
Morocco — 12, 25, 32, 8
Netherlands — 9*, 42, 100

World average — 19, 40, 52, 95

New Zealand — 16, 42, 66, 100
Pakistan — 13*, 31, 33, 99
Poland — 35*, 52, 83, 99
Portugal — 30*, 56, 81, 97
Saudi Arabia — 20*, 35, 41, 98
Somalia — 0*, 7, 29, 94
Spain — 18*, 57, 96
Sudan — 2, 21, 31, 44

Syria — 8*, 23, 55, 97
Turkey — 25*, 35, 42, 98
UK — 78
USA — 26, 47, 84
USSR — 37, 71, 100
Venezuela — 17*, 50, 98
Vietnam — 22, 58, 66, 100
Yugoslavia — 24, 49, 70, 95

Sources in Notes

# FEMINIST VOICES

Countries with feminist media and media services, 1985

| | | | | | |
|---|---|---|---|---|---|
| periodicals | presses publishers | bookstores | news services | radio television | film/video /cable |

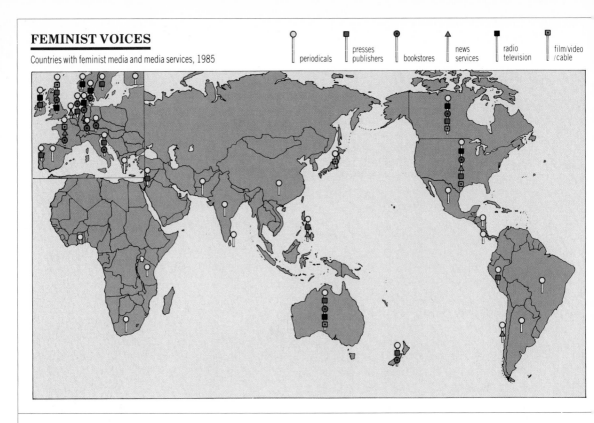

# MEDIA WORKERS

Women as a proportion of workers in the media where known, most recent year since 1970s, *percentages*

women in all media
women in broadcast management
women in print media

Bangladesh 1
Peru, Japan 2
Haiti, Honduras 5
Surinam, Guatemala, Pakistan, South Korea 10
Dominican Republic, Guyana, Mexico, 15
Trinidad & Tobago, Hong Kong, Malaysia 15
Sri Lanka 20
Ecuador 25
Costa Rica, Chile, Taiwan, Venezuela 35
Cuba, Thailand, USA 40
Australia 0
Austria 2
Ghana 3
Norway 4
Finland 6

Canada 7
UK 16
Sweden 30
Singapore 38
Jamaica 50
Japan 1
S. Korea 2
Pakistan, Southern India 3
Kenya 5
Morocco, Sudan, 10
Syria, Turkey 10
Norway, Denmark, West Germany 15
Sierra Leone 19
Egypt, Israel 20
Austria 27

# UP FRONT

Front-page stories written by women, USA, 1985, *percentages*

| | | | | | | | |
|---|---|---|---|---|---|---|---|
| USA Today | 41.5 | Detroit Free Press | 26.2 | Philadelphia Inquirer | 18.4 |
| Boston Globe | 30.5 | Cleveland Plain Dealer | 22.6 | Los Angeles Times | 17.7 |
| Atlanta Journal | 30.1 | Chicago Tribune | 19.2 | New York Times | 10.0 |
| Washington Post | 26.3 | Wall Street Journal | 18.8 | | |

Copyright © Pluto Press

Radio, television, newspapers and magazines entertain and educate. They are also important means for maintaining or changing the status quo. The mass media are growing rapidly, but small media are flourishing, too. Mass media means male media.

Women's media image is predominantly passive, domestic and, especially in advertisements, sexual. Women's news is considered to be fashion, style, social trends. Women do not appear to make the news, either as features or writers. Women working in the media are predominantly in low-paid, low-status jobs.

There is a growing feminist media addressing the concerns of women worldwide, but it is small compared to the reach of traditional women's media. Most pervasive of all are the sex magazines for men: a highly profitable industry selling a perverse, widely accepted image of women.

## THE FURTHEST REACH

Circulation by place of publication of selected magazines, mid-1980s, *thousands*

**MAINSTREAM WOMEN'S MAGAZINES**

7004 — Family Circle (USA)
6224 — McCall's (USA)
5123 — Ladies Home Journal (USA)
2257 — Woman's Own (UK)
1109 — Vogue (USA)
937 — Glamour (USA)
1661 — Bella (West Germany)
870 — House Beautiful (USA)
1235 — Australian Women's Weekly
400 — Brides (USA)
270 — Cosmopolitan (France)
1701 — Woman (UK)
210 — Cosmopolitan (Italy)
105 — Cosmopolitan (Netherlands)
221 — Fair Lady (South Africa)
45 — Eve's Weekly (India)
30 — Her World (Singapore)

**FEMINIST MAGAZINES**

463 — Ms (USA)
300 — Emma (West Germany)
70 — Courage (West Germany)
50 — Sojourner (USA)
30 — Spare Rib (UK)
10 — Manushi (India)
7 — Signs (USA)
5 — ISIS Women's World (Italy)
4 — Broadsheet (New Zealand)
3 — Connexions (USA)
1 — WIN News (USA)

**MEN'S SEX MAGAZINES**

6400 — Penthouse (international)
4700 — Playboy (international)
1500 — Hustler (USA)
500 — Gallery (USA)
400 — Forum (USA)

## FANTASY WORLD

Circulation of Playboy, all editions, 1985–86, *thousands*

4100 — American
477 — West German
265 — Japanese
210 — Brazilian
150 — Dutch
145 — French
140 — Mexican
77 — Australian
75 — Greek
70 — Argentinian
60 — Italian
55 — Hong Kong
35 — Spanish

Sources in Notes

# BODY BEAUTIFUL

Women's cosmetic surgery and percentage increase, USA, 1981-84

number of operations, 1984 — percentage increase since 1981

| | | |
|---|---|---|
| 59,120 — 31 | eye changes | |
| 56,400 — 30 | nose changes | |
| 43,200 — 39 | face-lifts | |
| 18,800 — 38 | dermabrasion | |
| 10,560 — 15 | ear changes | |
| 95,000 — 32 | breast enlargement | |
| 16,200 — 26 | breast lift | |
| 20,900 — 37 | tummy tuck | |
| 55,900 | fat removal (suction) | |
| 16,000 | surgical body contour | |

GREENLAND

1985 ICELAND

1961 1956

1959 1962

1961 1964

1965 1983
United Kingdom

1953 1953

1974 1969

1952 1975 1957
Finland

1955 1966 1984

1951 1952 1977
Sweden

1973 Athens
1971
Lebanon

1964

1954
EGYPT

1976
Israel

UNION OF SOVIET SOCIALIST REPUBLICS

MONGOLIA

CHINA

1966
INDIA

1976
Hong Kong

1965

1979
Perth

## THE BEAUTY BUSINESS

World cosmetic sales, 1984-85, $ billion

| 2.6 | 2.4 | 1.9 | 1.5 |
|-----|-----|-----|-----|
| Avon | Revlon | L'Oreal | Shiseido |

1978 1958 1974

## SOME NATIONAL BEAUTY CONTESTS

| USA • children | Miss Black America | Miss America Teenager | National Lollipop Queen • |
|---|---|---|---|
| Miss America | Miss Senior America | Miss Teen All-American | Most Beautiful Girl in the World |
| Miss USA | Miss Indian America | Miss Lovely Legs | UK • children |
| Mrs America | Miss Wheelchair America | Face of the Eighties | Miss Look of Radiance |
| Miss Nude America | Miss Deaf America | Maid of Cotton | Look of the Eighties |
| | | Miss Avocado | Miss Pears • |
| | | Little Miss Lovely • | European Queen of Beauty |

Copyright © Pluto Press

The quest for beauty is used to exalt and to degrade women, and as a distraction from reality. Presented as entertainment it has been turned into a serious preoccupation. Beauty contests attempt to create a fantasy world where women are meant to be ogled and men are polite voyeurs. These contests can be seen as simply part of the pornography continuum.

International beauty contests promote the export of culturally-specific notions of beauty that women everywhere are expected to meet: mostly, a white, European standard. The idea of women as beauty-objects transcends economic and political differences: rich and poor countries, communist and capitalist, all participate in the beauty beat.

Beauty is big business. Beauty contests are very profitable, and more are spawned each year. The cosmetics market is enormous. The demand for cosmetic surgery grows yearly.

THE TWO MAJOR INTERNATIONAL BEAUTY CONTESTS, 1985

- participants in both Miss World and Miss Universe
- participants in Miss World only
- participants in Miss Universe only
- other countries

Miss World winner (with date)
Miss Universe winner (with date)
Miss World site (permanent)
Miss Universe site (with date)

Sources in Notes

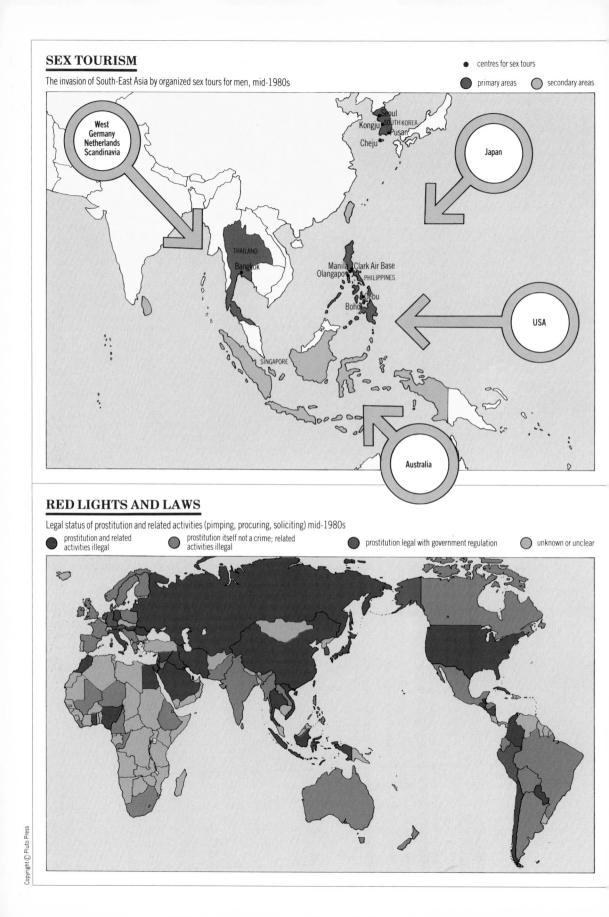

# SEX TOURISM

The invasion of South-East Asia by organized sex tours for men, mid-1980s

● centres for sex tours
● primary areas
● secondary areas

West
Germany
Netherlands
Scandinavia

Seoul
SOUTH KOREA
Kongju
Cheju
Pusan

Japan

THAILAND
Bangkok

Manila Clark Air Base
Olangapo
PHILIPPINES
Cebu
Bohol

USA

SINGAPORE

Australia

# RED LIGHTS AND LAWS

Legal status of prostitution and related activities (pimping, procuring, soliciting) mid-1980s

● prostitution and related
activities illegal
● prostitution itself not a crime; related
activities illegal
● prostitution legal with government regulation
● unknown or unclear

Copyright © Pluto Press

Prostitution is not a women's institution. It has always been controlled by men and sustained by violence. The image of the 'happy hooker' has little to do with reality. Poverty drives most women who 'choose' prostitution. Many girls are sold into prostitution by poor families. Once in the system, it is hard to get out.

In the international prostitution network, women are commodities. Prostitutes are traded, girls are bought and exchanged among pimps, marriage catalogues offer women for sale. Despite growing protests and exposure, the trade is flourishing and widespread.

Sex tours to South-East Asia for men represent an extreme of exploitation for women.

Prostitution exists in all countries, regardless of its legal status – but under different laws the treatment of prostitutes varies widely.

## INTERNATIONAL TRAFFIC IN WOMEN

Women being bought, sold and traded, as determined by major cases exposed from the mid-1970s (internal trafficking not included)

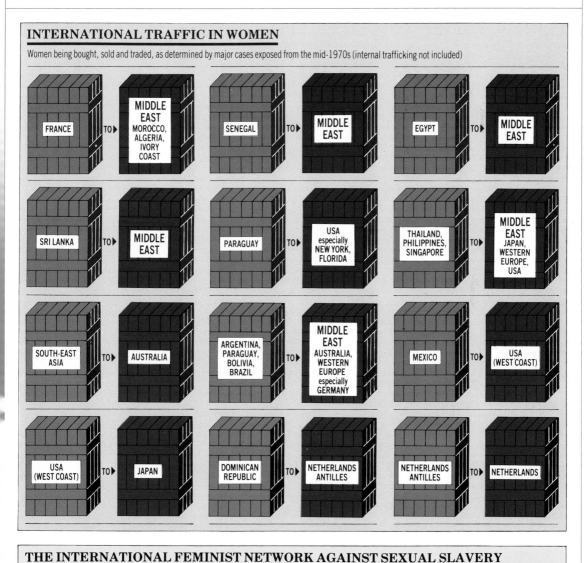

FRANCE TO▶ MIDDLE EAST MOROCCO, ALGERIA, IVORY COAST

SENEGAL TO▶ MIDDLE EAST

EGYPT TO▶ MIDDLE EAST

SRI LANKA TO▶ MIDDLE EAST

PARAGUAY TO▶ USA especially NEW YORK, FLORIDA

THAILAND, PHILIPPINES, SINGAPORE TO▶ MIDDLE EAST JAPAN, WESTERN EUROPE, USA

SOUTH-EAST ASIA TO▶ AUSTRALIA

ARGENTINA, PARAGUAY, BOLIVIA, BRAZIL TO▶ MIDDLE EAST AUSTRALIA, WESTERN EUROPE especially GERMANY

MEXICO TO▶ USA (WEST COAST)

USA (WEST COAST) TO▶ JAPAN

DOMINICAN REPUBLIC TO▶ NETHERLANDS ANTILLES

NETHERLANDS ANTILLES TO▶ NETHERLANDS

## THE INTERNATIONAL FEMINIST NETWORK AGAINST SEXUAL SLAVERY

Countries with active participants, 1983

| | | | |
|---|---|---|---|
| Australia | France | Netherlands Antilles | Tahiti |
| Brazil | West Germany | Peru | Thailand |
| Cameroon | India | Philippines | USA |
| Colombia | Japan | Sri Lanka | Zimbabwe |
| Dominican Republic | Lebanon | Sweden | |
| Egypt | Netherlands | Switzerland | |

# SEX AND RAPE OFFENCES

Officially reported rape and sex offences, number per 100,000 population, mid-1970s

| | | | | |
|---|---|---|---|---|
| ○ 5 and below | ● 5.1-15 | ● 15.1-35 | ● 35.1-90 | ○ unclear or unknown |

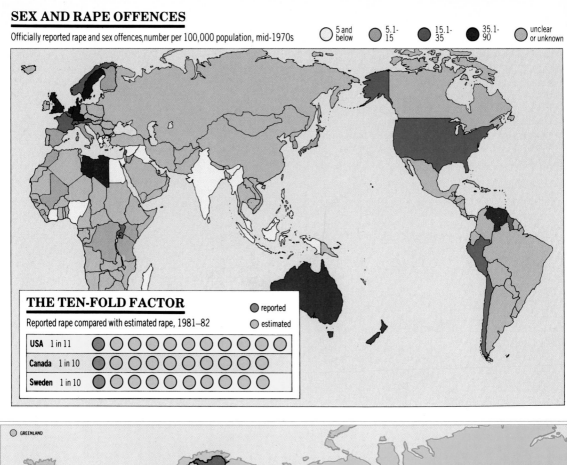

## THE TEN-FOLD FACTOR

Reported rape compared with estimated rape, 1981–82

● reported  ○ estimated

| USA | 1 in 11 | ●○○○○○○○○○○ |
|---|---|---|
| Canada | 1 in 10 | ●○○○○○○○○○○ |
| Sweden | 1 in 10 | ●○○○○○○○○○ |

## WIFE RAPE LAWS
### 1985

○ wife rape a crime during cohabitation

● wife rape while cohabiting not a crime, prosecutable only if separated or divorced

● wife rape never a crime

○ unknown or unclear

Copyright © Pluto Press

Rape is probably the most under-reported, fastest growing and least convicted crime in the world. It has long been considered as only a crime against property – the woman as man's property. Now it is beginning to be recognized for what it is: a crime of violence and power, and a violation of women's civil rights.

Men of all ages and backgrounds rape women of all ages and backgrounds. Women everywhere live under the threat of rape, especially in their own homes. Rape in families is not a secret any more: wife-rape is now prosecutable in parts of Europe and the USA, and is slowly being recognized as a crime elsewhere. Grass-roots organizing by women has brought about these legal and social changes, including the setting up of rape-crisis centres.

But in most countries, rape is still not properly recognized as a serious problem for women.

## OUT OF THE SHADOWS

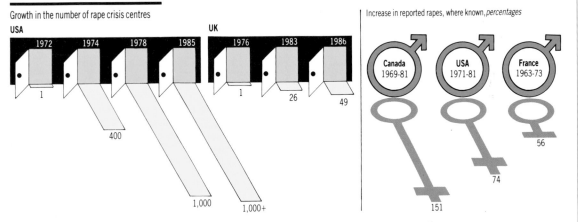

Growth in the number of rape crisis centres

Increase in reported rapes, where known, *percentages*

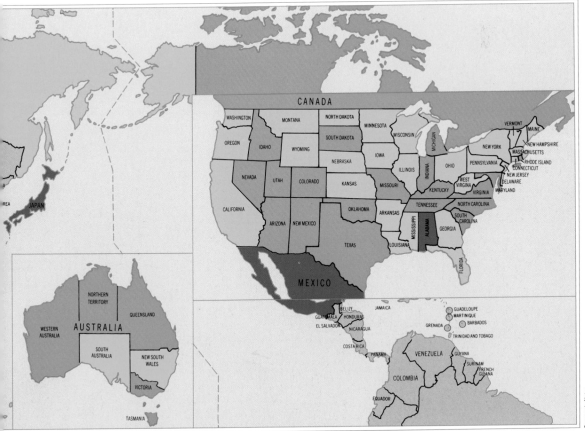

The women's movement has affected government and bureaucratic machinery internationally. Agendas now routinely include women's issues, and policy-making groups have women's advisory boards. These changes are often made reluctantly and may be primarily symbolic, but they are steps towards some improvement of women's status.

Ironically, channels of change for women are often not run by women. In most cases, women are barely represented in policy-making posts in governments or agencies, even those dealing mostly with women's issues.

Often the most effective channels are those that women set up themselves. Organizing by women is not new, but has certainly accelerated in the past decade. Conferences, international networks, non-government organizations and political action groups are at the forefront of change.

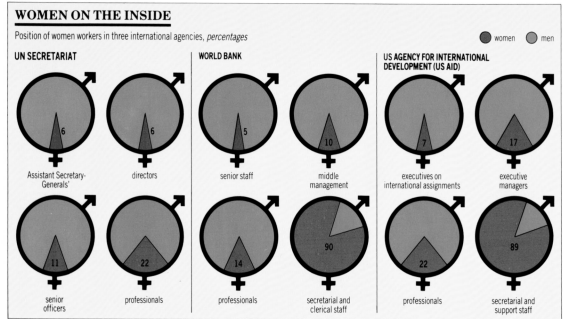

## WOMEN ON THE INSIDE

Position of women workers in three international agencies, *percentages*

● women  ● men

**UN SECRETARIAT**

6 — Assistant Secretary-Generals'
6 — directors
11 — senior officers
22 — professionals

**WORLD BANK**

5 — senior staff
10 — middle management
14 — professionals
90 — secretarial and clerical staff

**US AGENCY FOR INTERNATIONAL DEVELOPMENT (US AID)**

7 — executives on international assignments
17 — executive managers
22 — professionals
89 — secretarial and support staff

## CONFERENCES

Representation of women by women in major international forums

### UN CONFERENCE ON POPULATION
Mexico City, 1984

> 'improving the status of women may be the most effective and efficient solution to the population crisis... The formulation of population policy should include the full participation of women'
> *quote from the platform*

- of 140 countries represented, one-third had no women delegates
- the 18 dignitaries in the opening platform party were all men
- only 16 countries had women-headed delegations
- only one country, Western Samoa, had a women-majority delegation

### INTERNATIONAL LABOR ORGANIZATION (ILO) ANNUAL CONFERENCES
The 1975 Annual Conference passed a resolution of equality of opportunity between men and women.
Women delegates/advisors to ILO conferences, *percentages*

| 1975 | 11 | 1980 | 11 |
|---|---|---|---|
| 1976 | 10 | 1981 | 10 |
| 1977 | 9 | 1982 | 9 |
| 1978 | 5 | 1983 | 10 |
| 1979 | 7 | 1984 | 9 |

### UN DECADE FOR WOMEN CONFERENCE, 1985
- one-third of the delegates were men
- 14 of the country delegations were headed by men
- one delegation (North Korea) consisted entirely of men

## GETTING TOGETHER

Women's international organizations and founding dates, selected examples

| | |
|---|---|
| 1880-1901 | World Women's Christian Temperance Union<br>International Council of Nurses<br>General Federation of Women's Clubs |
| 1900-1915 | International Council of Jewish Women<br>International Alliance of Women<br>Women's International League for Peace and Freedom<br>International Federation for Home Economics |
| 1916-1930 | Associated Country Women of the World<br>International Conference of Midwives<br>International Federation of Business and Professional Women<br>International Federation of University Women<br>Medical Women's International Association<br>Zonta International |
| 1931-1945 | International Federation of Women Lawyers<br>Women's International Democratic Federation |
| 1946-1970 | All African Women's Conference<br>Federation of Asian Women's Associations<br>International Union of Women Architects<br>World Movement of Mothers |
| 1970-1985 | Arab Women Solidarity Association<br>International Women's Studies Association<br>International Network Against Female Sexual Slavery<br>Conference of Non-Governmental Organizations |

Copyright © Pluto Press

## GOVERNMENT CHANNELS

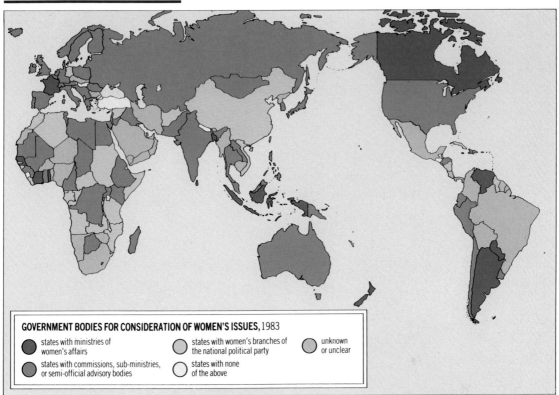

**GOVERNMENT BODIES FOR CONSIDERATION OF WOMEN'S ISSUES,** 1983

○ states with ministries of women's affairs

○ states with commissions, sub-ministries, or semi-official advisory bodies

○ states with women's branches of the national political party

○ states with none of the above

○ unknown or unclear

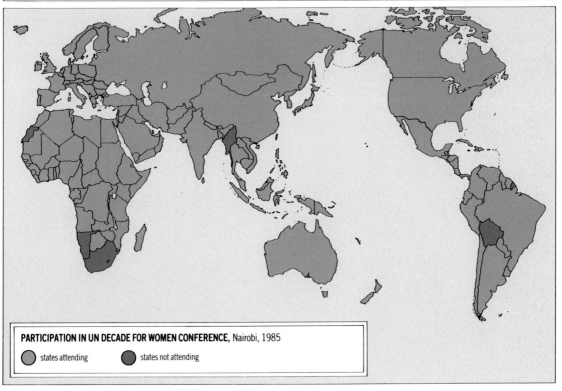

**PARTICIPATION IN UN DECADE FOR WOMEN CONFERENCE,** Nairobi, 1985

○ states attending   ○ states not attending

CONTRACEPTIVES MANUFACTURER FACES LEGAL CHARGES . . . . . . .
WOMEN'S MARCH FOR PEACE . . . . . WOMEN PROTEST PORNOGRAPHY
FILM . . . . . WOMEN PRESS CHARGES OF SEXUAL HARRASSMENT . . .
SARI SQUAD PROTESTS DEPORTATION . . . NURSES ON STRIKE . . .
WOMEN PROTEST DAYCARE CUTBACKS . . . TEXTILE WORKERS WALK OUT

## WOMEN'S PEACE CAMPS

1970-85

♀ Mt Fuji, Japan

♀ peace camps

Copyright © Pluto Press

Women engage in many forms of protest: by challenging conventions in their marriages and workplaces; by opening battered women's refuges and women's bookstores; by starting alternative healthcare networks. Sometimes they take to the streets to make their voices heard on issues of violence, pornography, abortion, social security and peace.

Nowhere is there much support for women, as such, to organize. In many countries, a women's

protest is in itself a major breakthrough, and flouts conventions of how women are supposed to behave. But almost all the advances in women's rights in the last century have been won only because women have been active on their own behalf.

Peace has always been a women's issue: women have been in the lead in anti-war and anti-militarist movements for the last century, as in the current women's peace camp movement.

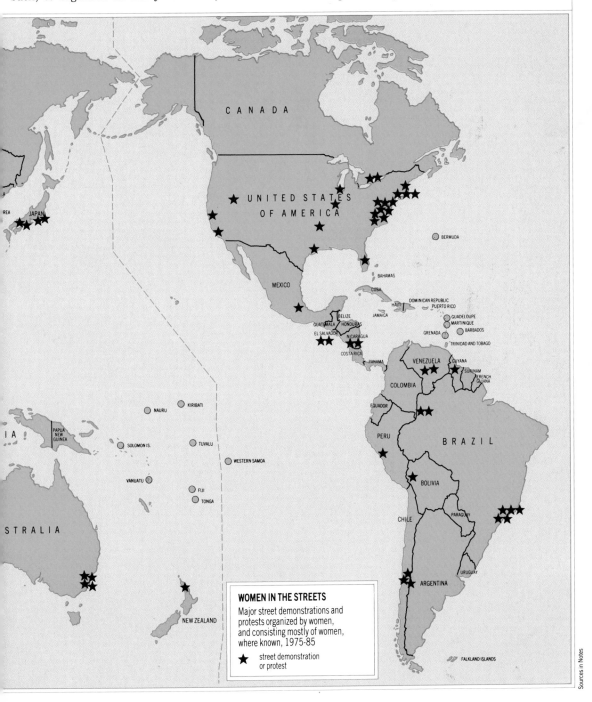

**WOMEN IN THE STREETS**

Major street demonstrations and protests organized by women, and consisting mostly of women, where known, 1975-85

★ street demonstration or protest

When official international agencies such as the United Nations gather statistics, they choose the subjects they consider important and accessible.

The statistics that exist on women reflect those choices. Information about women's fertility and use of contraceptives is considered critical, but data on maternal mortality is not. Similarly, conventional labour force statistics on women are systematically gathered, but data on women's unpaid labour is collected only sporadically. The 'official' woman is thus an incomplete one. Many aspects of her life are invisible including domestic violence, rape and poverty. Feminists and their organizations are still virtually the only sources for this officially unimportant information. Even when governments and agencies have the opportunity to collect or publish gender-specific data they sometimes choose not to.

Men in power still ignore women in numbers.

## BODY CHARTS

How 76 governments collect data on health, by region, 1985, *percentages*

ALL

AFRICA

54 · 70

51 · 57

41

5

34

15

☐ collected by sex
▦ proportion of those collected that are also published by sex
▨ not collected by sex
▓ not collected

AMERICAS

41 · 73

53

6

ASIA

41 · 85

59

EUROPE

76 · 75

24

## INVISIBLE WOMEN

Parts of women's lives not recorded in the standard international sources, mid-1980s

| | | | | | |
|---|---|---|---|---|---|
| child marriage | see map 2 | time use and the division of labour | see map 13 | military service | see map 32 |
| domestic violence | 3 | migration for work | 17 | media | 34 |
| genital mutilation | 4 | job ghettos | 18 | beauty contests | 35 |
| polygyny | 5 | land rights | 21 | sexual slavery and prostitution | 36 |
| reproductive technology | 6 | university admissions | 23 | rape and wife rape | 37 |
| sterilization abuse | 7 | women refugees | 27 | women's organizations | 38 |
| illegal abortion and attacks on abortion | 9 | feminization of poverty | 28 | protests | 39 |

Copyright © Pluto Press

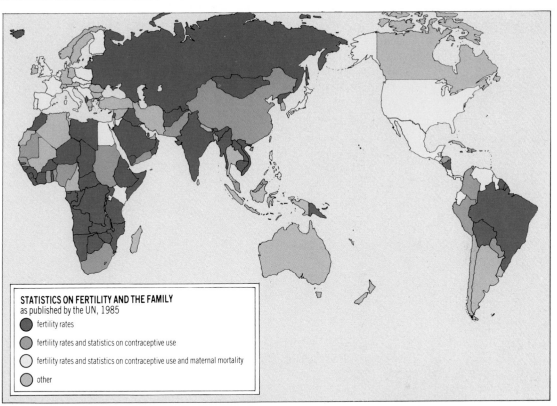

**STATISTICS ON FERTILITY AND THE FAMILY**
as published by the UN, 1985

- fertility rates
- fertility rates and statistics on contraceptive use
- fertility rates and statistics on contraceptive use and maternal mortality
- other

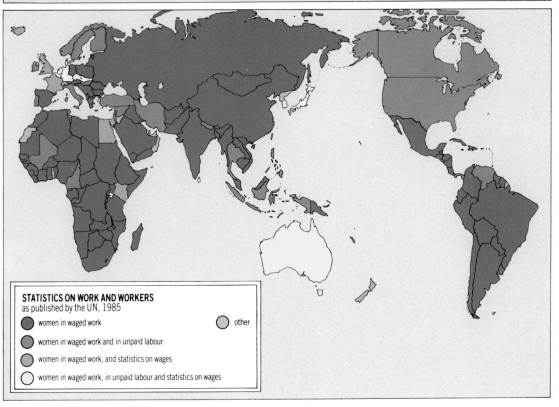

**STATISTICS ON WORK AND WORKERS**
as published by the UN, 1985

- women in waged work
- women in waged work and in unpaid labour
- women in waged work, and statistics on wages
- women in waged work, in unpaid labour and statistics on wages
- other

F = female  M = mal[e]

| | Population 000s 1985 | | Rural population percentages 1980 | | Population over 60 years percentages 1980 | | Marriage minimum legal age with parental consent | | Children per mother average number | Contraceptiv[e] use by women percentages |
|---|---|---|---|---|---|---|---|---|---|---|
| | F | M | F | M | F | M | F | M | | |
| Afghanistan | 7141 | 7495 | 42 | 43 | 4 | 4 | 16 | 18 | 6.9 | 2 |
| Albania | 1505 | 1545 | 32 | 31 | 8 | 6 | NA | | NA | NA |
| Algeria | 11000 | 11000 | 20 | 20 | 6 | 5 | 16 | 18 | 7.0 | <15 |
| Angola | 4448 | 4306 | 42 | 37 | 5 | 5 | NA | | 6.5 | 1 |
| Antigua and Barbuda | 34 | 31 | NA | | 10 | 6 | NA | | 2.5 | NA |
| Argentina | 15400 | 15200 | 8 | 10 | 14 | 11 | 16 | 18 | 3.4 | 40–59 |
| Australia | 7835 | 7879 | 5 | 6 | 16 | 13 | 16 | 18 | 2.1 | 72 |
| Austria | 3920 | 3567 | 23 | 22 | 24 | 15 | 16 | 19 | 1.6 | >60 |
| Bahamas | 106 | 104 | NA | | 7 | 6 | NA | | 2.5 | NA |
| Bahrain | 177 | 254 | 11 | 11 | 4 | 3 | NA | | 5.2 | <15 |
| Bangladesh | 49000 | 52100 | 43 | 45 | 5 | 5 | 16 | 18 | 6.6 | 12 |
| Barbados | 138 | 127 | 31 | 30 | 15 | 11 | 16 | 16 | 2.6 | 30 |
| Belgium | 5032 | 4848 | 14 | 14 | 22 | 17 | 15 | 18 | 1.6 | 76 |
| Belize | 60 | 60 | NA | | 7 | 6 | NA | | 4.5 | <15 |
| Benin | 2038 | 1967 | 35 | 34 | 5 | 4 | None | | 7.0 | 1 |
| Bermuda | NA | | NA | | NA | | NA | | NA | NA |
| Bhutan | 686 | 731 | 47 | 49 | 6 | 5 | NA | | 6.1 | <15 |
| Bolivia | 3232 | 3139 | 34 | 33 | 6 | 5 | 12 | 14 | 6.8 | <15 |
| Botswana | 564 | 515 | 39 | 32 | 4 | 3 | NA | | 6.5 | 8 |
| Brazil | 67900 | 67700 | 16 | 17 | 7 | 6 | 16 | 18 | 4.2 | 40–59 |
| Brunei | 93 | 107 | NA | | 4 | 4 | NA | | NA | 15–39 |
| Bulgaria | 4637 | 4583 | 18 | 18 | 19 | 16 | 18 | 18 | 2.2 | 40–59 |
| Burkina | 3507 | 3432 | 46 | 45 | 5 | 4 | NA | | 6.5 | 1 |
| Burma | 19800 | 19700 | 37 | 36 | 6 | 6 | NA | | 5.5 | <15 |
| Burundi | 2372 | 2260 | 50 | 48 | 6 | 5 | NA | | 6.5 | 1 |
| Cameroon | 4932 | 4782 | 34 | 31 | 7 | 6 | 15 | 18 | 6.4 | 1 |
| Canada | 12900 | 12700 | 12 | 13 | 15 | 12 | 16 | 16 | 1.8 | 68 |
| Cape Verde | 162 | 159 | 48 | 47 | 7 | 6 | NA | | 3.0 | NA |
| CAR | 1324 | 1243 | 31 | 28 | 7 | 5 | 16 | 18 | 5.9 | <15 |
| Chad | 2547 | 2472 | 42 | 40 | 6 | 5 | NA | | 5.9 | 1 |
| Chile | 6096 | 5979 | 9 | 10 | 9 | 7 | 12 | 14 | 3.1 | 43 |
| China | 521000 | 542000 | 37 | 38 | 9 | 7 | 20 | 22 | 2.3 | 70 |
| Colombia | 14300 | 14400 | 14 | 16 | 6 | 5 | 14 | 16 | 3.6 | 52 |
| Comoros | 231 | 226 | 45 | 43 | 5 | 4 | NA | | 6.2 | NA |
| Congo | 882 | 858 | 33 | 30 | 6 | 5 | NA | | 5.9 | <15 |
| Costa Rica | 1287 | 1313 | 27 | 30 | 6 | 5 | 15 | 15 | 3.7 | 64 |
| Cuba | 4925 | 5113 | 16 | 19 | 11 | 11 | 14 | 16 | 2.1 | 40–59 |
| Cyprus | 334 | 333 | 27 | 26 | 15 | 13 | 16 | 18 | 2.3 | NA |
| Czechoslovakia | 7996 | 7652 | 19 | 18 | 19 | 14 | 18 | 18 | 2.3 | 66 |
| Denmark | 2608 | 2536 | 7 | 8 | 22 | 18 | 18 | 18 | 1.5 | 67 |
| Djibouti | NA | | NA | | NA | | NA | | NA | <15 |
| Dominica | NA | | NA | | NA | | NA | | 3.4 | NA |
| Dominican Republic | 3101 | 3142 | 23 | 26 | 5 | 5 | 15 | 16 | 4.2 | 43 |

A = not available

| Maternal mortality deaths per 100,000 live births | Proportion of women in labour force percentages | Labour force percentages | | Agricultural labour force percentages | | Proportion of girls in secondary education percentages | Illiteracy percentages | | Life expectancy at birth years | | Anaemia during pregnancy percentages | Right to vote won by women year |
|---|---|---|---|---|---|---|---|---|---|---|---|---|
| | | F | M | F | M | | F | M | F | M | | |
| NA | 21 | 18 | 88 | 3 | 97 | 4 | 94 | 67 | 37.3 | 36.6 | NA | 1964 |
| NA | 59 | 40 | 60 | 50 | 50 | 60 | NA | | 71.5 | 68 | NA | 1946 |
| NA | 7 | 9 | 91 | 5 | 95 | 29 | 87 | 58 | 56.3 | 54.4 | 65 | 1958 |
| 13 | 9 | 9 | 91 | 47 | 53 | 6 | NA | | 41.6 | 38.5 | NA | 1975 |
| NA | 29 | NA | | NA | | NA | NA | | NA | | NA | 1951 |
| 8 | 29 | 27 | 73 | 4 | 96 | 60 | 8 | 7 | 72.1 | 65.4 | 61 | 1947 |
| 0 | 48 | 38 | 62 | 24 | 76 | 88 | 0 | 0 | 77 | 70.1 | NA | 1902 |
| 0 | 49 | 39 | 61 | 48 | 52 | 76 | <1 | <1 | 75.6 | 68.5 | NA | 1919 |
| 1 | 34 | NA | | NA | | 79 | <10 | <10 | NA | | NA | 1962 |
| NA | 15 | 11 | 89 | NA | | 52 | 30 | 15 | 68.1 | 64.1 | NA | |
| NA | 13 | 17 | 83 | 4 | 69 | 6 | 87 | 63 | 46.1 | 47.1 | 66 | 1956 |
| 3 | 63 | 46 | 54 | 48 | 52 | 85 | <1 | <1 | 73.2 | 67.9 | NA | 1951 |
| 2 | 48 | 37 | 63 | 26 | 74 | 89 | <1 | <1 | 75.7 | 69.1 | NA | 1948 |
| NA | NA | NA | | NA | | NA | 9 | 9 | NA | | NA | 1954 |
| NA | 40 | 36 | 64 | 21 | 79 | 8 | 83 | 60 | 42.1 | 39.0 | NA | 1956 |
| NA | 72 | 45 | 55 | NA | | NA | 1 | 2 | NA | | NA | 1944 |
| NA | NA | NA | | 40 | 60 | 5 | NA | | 43.1 | 44.6 | NA | |
| NA | 22 | 22 | 78 | 27 | 73 | 31 | 49 | 24 | 50.9 | 46.5 | NA | 1952 |
| NA | 44 | 40 | 60 | 95 | 5 | 23 | 56 | 63 | 54.2 | 50.8 | NA | 1966 |
| NA | 29 | 27 | 73 | 15 | 85 | 35 | 26 | 22 | 64.3 | 59.5 | 20 | 1932 |
| NA | 27 | 24 | 76 | 28 | 72 | NA | 50 | 25 | NA | | NA | NA |
| 9 | 67 | 43 | 57 | 58 | 42 | 83 | 8 | 3 | 73.8 | 68.7 | NA | 1947 |
| NA | 81 | 43 | 57 | 46 | 54 | 2 | 97 | 85 | 41.6 | 38.5 | NA | 1956 |
| NA | 46 | 36 | 64 | 25 | 75 | 18 | 44 | 24 | 54.1 | 51 | 55 | 1935 |
| NA | 95 | 53 | 47 | 56 | 44 | 2 | 85 | 61 | 43.6 | 40.4 | NA | 1961 |
| NA | 52 | 38 | 62 | 92 | 8 | 12 | 76 | 45 | 47.6 | 44.4 | NA | 1956 |
| 7 | 56 | 41 | 59 | 25 | 75 | 90 | 0 | 0 | 78.1 | 70.5 | NA | 1920 |
| 34 | NA | NA | | 19 | 81 | NA | NA | | 56.2 | 53.1 | 42 | 1975 |
| NA | 83 | 48 | 52 | 52 | 48 | 7 | 81 | 52 | 42.6 | 39.4 | NA | 1956 |
| NA | 28 | 24 | 76 | 27 | 73 | 1 | 99 | 64 | 42.6 | 39.4 | NA | 1956 |
| 3 | 30 | 30 | 70 | 4 | 96 | 59 | 12 | 10 | 69 | 62.4 | 32 | 1949 |
| NA | 55 | 36 | 64 | 47 | 53 | 27 | 37 | 14 | 66.5 | 62.6 | NA | 1947 |
| 34 | 27 | 38 | 62 | 14 | 86 | 49 | 20 | 18 | 64.5 | 60 | 22 | 1957 |
| NA | NA | NA | | 34 | 66 | 17 | 48 | 34 | 49.7 | 46.4 | NA | NA |
| NA | 43 | 37 | 63 | 34 | 66 | 53 | 49 | 25 | 46.1 | 43 | NA | 1956 |
| 37 | 25 | 25 | 75 | 5 | 95 | 51 | 12 | 11 | 74 | 69 | 44 | 1949 |
| 53 | 36 | 31 | 69 | 15 | 85 | 77 | 5 | 4 | 74.4 | 71.1 | NA | 1934 |
| NA | 46 | 39 | 61 | 59 | 41 | 66 | 17 | 4 | 75.5 | 72 | NA | 1959 |
| 3 | 71 | 47 | 53 | 42 | 58 | 56 | 0 | 0 | 74.1 | 67 | NA | 1919 |
| 5 | 72 | 45 | 55 | 24 | 76 | 85 | 0 | 0 | 77.3 | 71.3 | NA | 1915 |
| NA | NA | NA | | NA | | NA | NA | | NA | | NA | 1957 |
| 15 | NA | 37 | 63 | 27 | 73 | NA | 6 | 6 | NA | | 46 | 1967 |
| 56 | 13 | 12 | 88 | 44 | 54 | 33 | 34 | 31 | 62.2 | 58.4 | NA | 1942 |

F = female M = male

| | Population 000s 1985 | | Rural population percentages 1980 | | Population over 60 years percentages 1980 | | Marriage minimum legal age with parental consent | | Children per mother average number | Contraceptive use by women percentages |
|---|---|---|---|---|---|---|---|---|---|---|
| | F | M | F | M | F | M | F | M | | |
| Ecuador | 4682 | 4698 | 27 | 29 | 5 | 5 | 12 | 14 | 6.3 | 6 |
| Egypt | 23000 | 23800 | 27 | 27 | 7 | 6 | 16 | 18 | 5.3 | 20 |
| El Salvador | 2764 | 2788 | 28 | 30 | 6 | 5 | 14 | 16 | 5.8 | 34 |
| Equatorial Guinea | 200 | 192 | 25 | 21 | 7 | 6 | NA | | 5.7 | <15 |
| Ethiopia | 18300 | 18200 | 44 | 41 | 4 | 4 | var. | | 6.5 | 1 |
| Fiji | 342 | 343 | 28 | 29 | 6 | 6 | 16 | 18 | 3.6 | 40 |
| Finland | 2518 | 2357 | 19 | 19 | 21 | 13 | 17 | 18 | 1.6 | 77 |
| France | 27800 | 26800 | 11 | 11 | 20 | 15 | 15 | 18 | 1.8 | 82 |
| French Guiana | NA | | NA | | NA | | NA | | NA | NA |
| French Polynesia | 55 | 58 | NA | | 4 | 5 | NA | | NA | NA |
| Gabon | 593 | 574 | 34 | 30 | 10 | 9 | 15 | 18 | 4.4 | <15 |
| The Gambia | 326 | 317 | 41 | 40 | 5 | 5 | None | | 6.4 | 1 |
| Germany, East | 8771 | 7871 | 12 | 11 | 24 | 14 | 18 | 18 | 1.8 | >60 |
| Germany, West | 31700 | 29400 | 7 | 8 | 24 | 15 | 16 | 16 | 1.4 | >60 |
| Ghana | 6804 | 6674 | 33 | 32 | 5 | 4 | None | 21 | 6.5 | 4 |
| Greece | 5049 | 4884 | 19 | 19 | 20 | 16 | 14 | 18 | 2.3 | >60 |
| Greenland | NA | | NA | | NA | | NA | | NA | >60 |
| Grenada | NA | | NA | | NA | | 16 | 16 | NA | NA |
| Guadeloupe | 164 | 156 | 28 | 29 | 12 | 10 | 15 | 18 | 3.0 | 44 |
| Guatemala | 4143 | 4260 | 29 | 32 | 5 | 5 | 14 | 16 | 5.7 | 19 |
| Guinea | 2747 | 2683 | 41 | 40 | 5 | 5 | 17 | 18 | 6.5 | 1 |
| Guinea–Bissau | 458 | 432 | 38 | 38 | 7 | 6 | NA | | 5.4 | 1 |
| Guyana | 476 | 478 | 39 | 40 | 6 | 6 | 14 | 16 | 3.9 | 31 |
| Haiti | 3337 | 3248 | 37 | 38 | 6 | 5 | None | | 4.6 | 5 |
| Honduras | 2181 | 2192 | 31 | 33 | 5 | 4 | 12 | 14 | 6.5 | 9 |
| Hong Kong | 2665 | 2944 | 5 | 5 | 13 | 10 | 16 | 16 | 2.1 | 72 |
| Hungary | 5552 | 5245 | 23 | 23 | 21 | 15 | 14 | 16 | 2.1 | 73 |
| Iceland | 119 | 123 | 5 | 6 | 15 | 12 | 18 | 18 | 2.3 | >60 |
| India | 367000 | 394000 | 38 | 40 | 6 | 6 | 18 | 21 | 5.0 | 16 |
| Indonesia | 82800 | 82100 | 40 | 39 | 6 | 5 | 16 | 19 | 4.8 | 26 |
| Iran | 22100 | 23000 | 25 | 25 | 5 | 5 | NA | | 6.0 | 24 |
| Iraq | 7725 | 7951 | 14 | 14 | 5 | 4 | 18 | 18 | 7.0 | 23 |
| Ireland | 1795 | 1800 | 20 | 22 | 16 | 13 | 16 | 16 | 3.5 | 60 |
| Israel | 2146 | 2152 | 5 | 6 | 13 | 11 | None | 16 | 3.5 | 40–59 |
| Italy | 29000 | 27800 | 15 | 15 | 21 | 17 | 16 | 18 | 1.9 | >60 |
| Ivory Coast | 4792 | 5006 | 31 | 31 | 5 | 5 | 15 | 18 | 6.7 | <15 |
| Jamaica | 1171 | 1152 | 29 | 30 | 9 | 8 | 16 | 16 | 3.9 | 38 |
| Japan | 61000 | 59100 | 11 | 11 | 16 | 12 | 16 | 18 | 1.9 | 65 |
| Jordan | 1699 | 1811 | 22 | 22 | 4 | 4 | 17 | 18 | 7.2 | 22 |
| Kampuchea | 3717 | 3677 | 43 | 43 | 5 | 4 | NA | | 4.1 | NA |
| Kenya | 10300 | 10300 | 44 | 41 | 3 | 3 | var. | | 8.2 | 7 |
| Korea, North | 10100 | 10000 | 20 | 20 | 7 | 5 | NA | | 4.5 | NA |
| Korea, South | 20300 | 20600 | 22 | 23 | 8 | 6 | 16 | 18 | 3.5 | 50 |

NA = not available

| Maternal mortality deaths per 100,000 live births | Proportion of women in labour force percentages | Labour force percentages | | Agricultural labour force percentages | | Proportion of girls in secondary education percentages | Illiteracy percentages | | Life expectancy at birth years | | Anaemia during pregnancy percentages | Right to vote won by women year |
|---|---|---|---|---|---|---|---|---|---|---|---|---|
| | | F | M | F | M | | F | M | F | M | | |
| 212 | 19 | 21 | 79 | 12 | 88 | 42 | 30 | 22 | 62 | 58 | NA | 1929 |
| 83 | 7 | 11 | 89 | 8 | 92 | 39 | 78 | 46 | 55.6 | 53.9 | 75 | 1956 |
| 36 | 42 | 35 | 65 | 23 | 77 | 23 | 41 | 35 | 64.5 | 60 | 15 | 1950 |
| NA | 4 | 5 | 95 | 3 | 97 | 4 | NA | | 43.6 | 40.4 | NA | |
| NA | 56 | 39 | 61 | 34 | 66 | 8 | 99 | 92 | 42.5 | 39.3 | 6 | 1955 |
| 50 | 13 | 13 | 87 | 8 | 92 | 64 | 20 | 16 | 73.1 | 69.5 | 68 | 1962 |
| 7 | 63 | 47 | 53 | 37 | 63 | 95 | 0 | 0 | 76.6 | 68 | NA | 1906 |
| 5 | 53 | 40 | 60 | 30 | 70 | 89 | 0 | 0 | 78 | 69.8 | NA | 1944 |
| 67 | 55 | NA | | NA | | NA | NA | | NA | | NA | NA |
| NA | NA | NA | | NA | | NA | NA | | NA | | NA | NA |
| NA | 54 | NA | | 44 | 56 | 23 | 45 | 28 | 48.7 | 45.4 | NA | 1956 |
| NA | 71 | 44 | 56 | 49 | 51 | 8 | 88 | 71 | 35 | 32 | 80 | 1961 |
| 20 | 72 | 46 | 56 | 43 | 57 | 84 | 0 | 0 | 74.6 | 68.8 | NA | 1919 |
| 24 | 50 | 39 | 61 | 48 | 52 | 90 | 0 | 0 | 75.8 | 69 | NA | 1919 |
| NA | 56 | 42 | 58 | 54 | 46 | 27 | 82 | 57 | 51.7 | 48.3 | 64 | 1955 |
| 7 | 34 | 31 | 69 | 40 | 60 | 76 | 24 | 7 | 75 | 71.3 | NA | 1952 |
| NA | NA | NA | | NA | | NA | NA | | NA | | NA | 1915 |
| 39 | NA | 38 | 92 | NA | | NA | 2 | 2 | NA | | NA | 1967 |
| 36 | 53 | 43 | 57 | 22 | 78 | NA | NA | | 71.8 | 66.5 | NA | 1944 |
| 102 | 13 | 15 | 85 | 6 | 94 | 15 | 62 | 46 | 58.8 | 56.9 | 34 | 1965 |
| NA | 59 | 41 | 59 | 44 | 56 | 9 | 96 | 66 | 39.8 | 36.7 | NA | 1956 |
| NA | 2 | 4 | 86 | 2 | 98 | 7 | 87 | 75 | 42.6 | 39.4 | 85 | 1973 |
| 104 | 26 | 25 | 75 | 10 | 90 | 61 | 11 | 6 | 68.9 | 64.1 | 55 | 1966 |
| NA | 54 | 41 | 59 | 53 | 47 | 12 | 83 | 74 | 52.2 | 49.1 | NA | 1950 |
| NA | 17 | 17 | 83 | 7 | 93 | 30 | 45 | 41 | 58.9 | 55.4 | NA | 1955 |
| 7 | 49 | 36 | 64 | 26 | 74 | 65 | 36 | 10 | NA | | NA | |
| 20 | 59 | 43 | 57 | 36 | 64 | 47 | 2 | 1 | 73.3 | 66.7 | NA | 1945 |
| 22 | 38 | 30 | 70 | 12 | 88 | 77 | NA | | 79.3 | 73.4 | NA | 1915 |
| NA | 30 | 26 | 74 | 24 | 76 | 20 | 81 | 52 | 50 | 51.2 | 68 | 1949 |
| NA | 39 | 33 | 67 | 33 | 67 | 22 | 55 | 31 | 51.3 | 48.7 | 65 | 1945 |
| NA | 14 | 14 | 86 | 12 | 88 | 32 | 76 | 52 | 58 | 58.4 | 50 | 1963 |
| NA | 4 | 4 | 96 | 37 | 63 | 38 | 77 | 37 | 60.9 | 57.2 | NA | 1964 |
| 5 | 34 | 30 | 70 | 10 | 90 | 98 | 7 | 4 | 74.6 | 69.6 | NA | 1922 |
| 10 | 38 | 37 | 63 | 19 | 81 | 78 | 17 | 7 | 74.9 | 71.4 | 29 | 1948 |
| 21 | 39 | 34 | 66 | 36 | 64 | 71 | 7 | 5 | 76.9 | 70.4 | NA | 1945 |
| NA | 75 | 41 | 59 | 81 | 19 | 8 | 76 | 55 | 49.6 | 43.4 | 34 | 1956 |
| 106 | 75 | 46 | 54 | 18 | 82 | 60 | 4 | 4 | 71 | 67 | 24 | 1944 |
| 23 | 54 | 38 | 62 | 48 | 52 | 92 | <1 | <1 | 78.3 | 73.1 | NA | 1945 |
| 50 | 6 | 7 | 93 | 1 | 99 | 66 | 46 | 19 | 62 | 58.3 | NA | 1982 |
| NA | NA | NA | | NA | | NA | 77 | 26 | 32.5 | 30 | NA | 1956 |
| 204 | 44 | 34 | 66 | 18 | 82 | 80 | 65 | 40 | 52.3 | 48.9 | 48 | 1963 |
| NA | 69 | 46 | 54 | 56 | 44 | NA | NA | | 64.6 | 60.5 | NA | 1946 |
| NA | 48 | 39 | 61 | 44 | 56 | 80 | 19 | 6 | 68.8 | 62.4 | NA | 1946 |

F = female  M = male

| | Population 000s 1985 | | Rural population percentages 1980 | | Population over 60 years percentages 1980 | | Marriage minimum legal age with parental consent | | Children per mother average number | Contraceptive use by women percentages |
|---|---|---|---|---|---|---|---|---|---|---|
| | F | M | F | M | F | M | F | M | | |
| Kuwait | 748 | 1038 | 6 | 6 | 3 | 3 | None | | 6.2 | <15 |
| Laos | 2195 | 2228 | 43 | 43 | 5 | 5 | NA | | 6.1 | NA |
| Lebanon | 1379 | 1289 | 12 | 12 | 8 | 8 | var. | | 3.8 | 57 |
| Lesotho | 783 | 736 | 48 | 48 | 6 | 5 | 16 | 18 | 5.8 | 5 |
| Liberia | 1105 | 1086 | 35 | 33 | 5 | 5 | 16 | 16 | 6.9 | 1 |
| Libya | 1705 | 1900 | 23 | 25 | 4 | 4 | var. | | 7.2 | <15 |
| Luxembourg | 183 | 179 | 11 | 11 | 22 | 16 | 15 | 18 | 1.5 | >60 |
| Macau | 121 | 128 | NA | | 8 | 6 | NA | | NA | NA |
| Madagascar | 5045 | 4967 | 42 | 40 | 6 | 5 | 14 | 17 | 6.5 | <15 |
| Malawi | 3601 | 3415 | 35 | 31 | 4 | 4 | NA | | 7.8 | 1 |
| Malaysia | 7711 | 7841 | 35 | 36 | 6 | 6 | 18 | 18 | 4.3 | 33 |
| Maldives | 68 | 75 | NA | | 3 | 5 | NA | | NA | NA |
| Mali | 4156 | 3897 | 41 | 39 | 5 | 4 | 15 | 18 | 6.7 | 1 |
| Malta | 199 | 183 | 8 | 8 | 15 | 12 | 14 | 16 | 2.0 | NA |
| Martinique | 161 | 152 | 16 | 17 | 13 | 11 | 15 | 18 | 2.6 | 51 |
| Mauritania | 954 | 935 | 32 | 32 | 5 | 4 | NA | | 6.9 | 1 |
| Mauritius | 531 | 519 | 24 | 24 | 7 | 5 | 15 | 18 | 3.1 | 52 |
| Mexico | 39400 | 39600 | 16 | 17 | 6 | 5 | 14 | 16 | 5.4 | 40 |
| Mongolia | 948 | 952 | 25 | 25 | 6 | 5 | NA | | 5.4 | NA |
| Morocco | 11800 | 11800 | 29 | 30 | 5 | 5 | var. | | 6.1 | 7 |
| Mozambique | 7144 | 6942 | 47 | 45 | 6 | 5 | NA | | 6.1 | <15 |
| Namibia | 781 | 769 | 29 | 26 | 6 | 5 | NA | | 6.1 | <15 |
| Nauru | NA | | NA | | NA | | NA | | NA | NA |
| Nepal | 8030 | 8453 | 47 | 48 | 5 | 5 | 16 | 18 | 6.5 | 3 |
| Netherlands | 7296 | 7211 | 12 | 12 | 19 | 15 | 16 | 18 | 1.6 | 64 |
| New Zealand | 1645 | 1646 | 7 | 8 | 15 | 12 | 16 | 16 | 2.2 | >60 |
| Nicaragua | 1636 | 1636 | 22 | 24 | 4 | 4 | 14 | 15 | 6.3 | 9 |
| Niger | 3086 | 3029 | 45 | 42 | 5 | 4 | 16 | 18 | 7.0 | 1 |
| Nigeria | 48100 | 47100 | 41 | 39 | 4 | 4 | var. | | 7.1 | <15 |
| Norway | 2092 | 2057 | 23 | 24 | 23 | 19 | 18 | 18 | 1.8 | 71 |
| Oman | 579 | 649 | NA | | 4 | 4 | NA | | 7.1 | <15 |
| Pakistan | 48900 | 52800 | 35 | 37 | 4 | 4 | 16 | 18 | 6.4 | 5 |
| Panama | 1069 | 1112 | 21 | 24 | 7 | 7 | 16 | 18 | 3.5 | 54 |
| Papua New Guinea | 1768 | 1928 | 36 | 36 | 5 | 5 | 16 | 18 | 6.3 | 3 |
| Paraguay | 1844 | 1838 | 29 | 31 | 6 | 5 | 12 | 14 | 5.2 | 24 |
| Peru | 9744 | 9923 | 16 | 16 | 6 | 5 | 14 | 16 | 5.4 | 31 |
| Philippines | 27100 | 27600 | 31 | 33 | 5 | 5 | 14 | 16 | 4.6 | 37 |
| Poland | 19200 | 18400 | 22 | 22 | 16 | 11 | 16 | 16 | 2.3 | 57 |
| Portugal | 5281 | 4796 | 36 | 34 | 17 | 13 | 16 | 16 | 2.3 | NA |
| Puerto Rico | 1774 | 1683 | 16 | 14 | 12 | 11 | NA | | 2.8 | 62 |
| Qatar | 102 | 199 | NA | | 5 | 4 | NA | | 6.8 | <15 |
| Reunion | 280 | 283 | 22 | 24 | 6 | 7 | NA | | 2.8 | NA |
| Romania | 11700 | 11400 | 26 | 26 | 16 | 12 | 16 | 18 | 2.4 | 40–59 |

| Maternal mortality deaths per 100,000 live births | Proportion of women in labour force percentages | Labour force percentages | | Agricultural labour force percentages | | Proportion of girls in secondary education percentages | Illiteracy percentages | | Life expectancy at birth years | | Anaemia during pregnancy percentages | Right to vote won by women year |
|---|---|---|---|---|---|---|---|---|---|---|---|---|
| | | F | M | F | M | | F | M | F | M | | |
| 5 | 19 | 13 | 87 | 1 | 99 | 70 | 66 | 35 | 71.6 | 66.9 | NA | |
| NA | 71 | 45 | 55 | 47 | 53 | 14 | 64 | 49 | 49 | 46.1 | 62 | 1956 |
| NA | 18 | 20 | 80 | 23 | 77 | 56 | 42 | 22 | 67 | 63.1 | 50 | 1957 |
| NA | 72 | 44 | 56 | 46 | 54 | 20 | 20 | 43 | 49 | 45.7 | NA | 1966 |
| NA | 39 | 31 | 69 | 88 | 12 | 11 | 88 | 70 | 48.7 | 45.4 | NA | 1946 |
| NA | 5 | 5 | 95 | 2 | 98 | 54 | 85 | 39 | 57 | 53.8 | 47 | 1963 |
| 50 | 39 | 33 | 67 | NA | | 66 | 0 | 0 | 75.7 | 68.2 | NA | 1918 |
| NA | NA | NA | | NA | | NA | NA | | NA | | NA | NA |
| NA | 74 | 45 | 55 | 91 | 9 | 10 | NA | | 48.5 | 47 | NA | 1956 |
| NA | 54 | 37 | 63 | 96 | 4 | 2 | 81 | 53 | 44.6 | 41.4 | 49 | 1964 |
| NA | 40 | 34 | 66 | 38 | 62 | 51 | 55 | 28 | 67.1 | 63.5 | 77 | 1957 |
| NA | 64 | 37 | 63 | NA | | NA | 18 | 18 | NA | | NA | NA |
| NA | 17 | 17 | 83 | 91 | 9 | 5 | 94 | 87 | 41.6 | 38.5 | 50 | 1956 |
| 30 | 22 | 24 | 76 | 12 | 88 | 63 | 18 | 12 | 73 | 68.4 | NA | 1947 |
| 27 | 56 | 45 | 55 | 24 | 76 | NA | NA | | 72.2 | 67.4 | NA | 1944 |
| NA | 4 | 4 | 96 | NA | | 4 | NA | | 43.6 | 40.4 | 24 | 1956 |
| 18 | 25 | 27 | 73 | 39 | 61 | 50 | 28 | 14 | 67.3 | 62.6 | 80 | 1958 |
| 19 | 21 | 20 | 80 | 9 | 91 | 49 | 20 | 12 | 66.3 | 61.9 | 38 | 1953 |
| NA | 43 | 33 | 67 | 36 | 64 | 92 | NA | | 64.6 | 60.5 | NA | 1924 |
| NA | 14 | 16 | 84 | 25 | 75 | 18 | 90 | 66 | 57 | 53.8 | 46 | 1959 |
| NA | 85 | 52 | 48 | 35 | 65 | 4 | 77 | 56 | 49.1 | 45.8 | NA | 1975 |
| NA | NA | NA | | NA | | NA | NA | | 47.5 | 45 | NA | 1966 |
| NA | NA | NA | | NA | | NA | NA | | NA | | NA | 1968 |
| NA | 45 | 35 | 65 | 39 | 61 | 9 | 95 | 67 | 43.1 | 44.6 | 33 | 1951 |
| | 39 | 34 | 66 | 15 | 85 | 91 | 0 | 0 | 78.6 | 72.1 | NA | 1919 |
| 3 | 44 | 34 | 66 | 22 | 78 | 82 | 0 | 0 | 75.7 | 69.3 | NA | 1893 |
| 5 | 25 | 22 | 78 | 8 | 92 | 47 | 43 | 42 | 57.3 | 55.3 | 20 | 1955 |
| NA | 11 | 10 | 90 | 11 | 89 | 2 | 94 | 86 | 42.1 | 39 | 57 | 1956 |
| NA | 53 | 40 | 60 | 35 | 65 | 6 | 77 | 55 | 48.1 | 44.9 | 65 | 1954 |
| | 66 | 41 | 59 | 31 | 69 | 95 | 0 | 0 | 78.6 | 72.2 | NA | 1913 |
| NA | NA | NA | | NA | | 7 | NA | | 48.4 | 46.2 | NA | |
| 0 | 11 | 12 | 88 | 3 | 97 | 8 | 90 | 70 | 47 | 49 | 65 | 1956 |
| 5 | 27 | 30 | 70 | 5 | 95 | 69 | 13 | 13 | 70.9 | 67.6 | NA | 1946 |
| NA | 70 | 41 | 59 | 46 | 54 | 7 | 76 | 61 | 50 | 50.5 | 55 | 1975 |
| 60 | 22 | 20 | 80 | 14 | 86 | 26 | 25 | 15 | 66.4 | 61.9 | NA | 1961 |
| 38 | 26 | 25 | 75 | 21 | 79 | 52 | 38 | 17 | 58.8 | 55.2 | 35 | 1955 |
| 41 | 53 | 39 | 61 | 27 | 73 | 68 | 19 | 16 | 64.3 | 60.9 | 47 | 1937 |
| 4 | 65 | 45 | 55 | 49 | 51 | 80 | 2 | 1 | 75 | 67 | NA | 1918 |
| 0 | 51 | 41 | 59 | 50 | 50 | 56 | 35 | 22 | 72.9 | 66.1 | NA | 1975 |
| 0 | 25 | 34 | 66 | 2 | 2 | NA | 13 | 11 | 77.1 | 70.3 | NA | 1936 |
| A | 2 | NA | | NA | | 77 | NA | | 71.6 | 66.7 | NA | |
| A | 37 | NA | | 4 | 96 | NA | NA | | 66.7 | 63 | NA | NA |
| 35 | 66 | 46 | 54 | 50 | 50 | 72 | 0 | 0 | 72.2 | 67.5 | NA | 1948 |

| | Population 000s 1985 | | Rural population percentages 1980 | | Population over 60 years percentages 1980 | | Marriage minimum legal age with parental consent | | Children per mother average number | Contraceptive use by women percentages |
|---|---|---|---|---|---|---|---|---|---|---|
| | F | M | F | M | F | M | F | M | | |
| Rwanda | 3098 | 3017 | 49 | 47 | 5 | 4 | NA | | 7.3 | <15 |
| St Christopher (St Kitts) – Nevis | 24 | 22 | NA | | 13 | 9 | NA | | 3.6 | NA |
| St Lucia | 64 | 57 | NA | | 9 | 6 | NA | | 4.5 | NA |
| St Vincent – Grenadines | NA | | NA | | NA | | 15 | 16 | 4.0 | NA |
| Sao Tome and Principe | NA | | NA | | NA | | NA | | 5.2 | NA |
| Saudi Arabia | 5104 | 6137 | 16 | 17 | 5 | 4 | 13 | 13 | 7.3 | <15 |
| Senegal | 3293 | 3227 | 38 | 37 | 5 | 4 | 16 | 20 | 6.5 | <15 |
| Seychelles | 32 | 32 | NA | | 11 | 7 | NA | | 4.2 | NA |
| Sierra Leone | 1837 | 1765 | 38 | 37 | 6 | 5 | None | | 6.5 | 6 |
| Singapore | 1263 | 1309 | 12 | 14 | 8 | 7 | 18 | 18 | 1.8 | 71 |
| Solomon Islands | 102 | 111 | NA | | 4 | 6 | NA | | NA | NA |
| Somalia | 3011 | 2541 | 38 | 32 | 8 | 5 | 16 | None | 6.5 | 1 |
| South Africa | 16300 | 16100 | 27 | 23 | 7 | 6 | 16 | 18 | 5.1 | <15 |
| Spain | 19900 | 19100 | 13 | 13 | 18 | 14 | 16 | 18 | 2.6 | 47 |
| Sri Lanka | 8054 | 8350 | 36 | 37 | 7 | 7 | var. | | 3.9 | 32 |
| Sudan | 10700 | 10800 | 37 | 38 | 5 | 4 | None | | 6.9 | <15 |
| Surinam | 179 | 174 | 28 | 28 | 7 | 6 | NA | | 4.6 | 15–39 |
| Swaziland | 332 | 317 | 46 | 45 | 5 | 4 | 16 | 18 | 6.5 | <15 |
| Sweden | 4177 | 4102 | 6 | 7 | 25 | 21 | 18 | 18 | 1.7 | 75 |
| Switzerland | 3207 | 3083 | 21 | 21 | 27 | 17 | 18 | 20 | 1.5 | >60 |
| Syria | 5203 | 5378 | 25 | 25 | 5 | 4 | | | 7.4 | 23 |
| Taiwan | NA | | NA | | NA | | NA | | 2.5 | 65 |
| Tanzania | 11400 | 11100 | 45 | 43 | 4 | 3 | 15 | 18 | 7.1 | <15 |
| Thailand | 25700 | 25900 | 43 | 43 | 6 | 5 | 17 | 17 | 3.9 | 52 |
| Togo | 1481 | 1442 | 42 | 41 | 5 | 5 | 17 | 20 | 6.1 | <15 |
| Trinidad and Tobago | 560 | 558 | 38 | 41 | 9 | 8 | var. | | 3.1 | 44 |
| Tunisia | 3583 | 3926 | 24 | 24 | 6 | 7 | 17 | 20 | 5.6 | 19 |
| Turkey | 24300 | 25700 | 27 | 25 | 7 | 6 | 15 | 17 | 5.0 | 40 |
| Uganda | 7916 | 7782 | 45 | 43 | 4 | 4 | 16 | 18 | 7.0 | <15 |
| United Arab Emirates | 411 | 901 | NA | | 5 | 3 | NA | | 6.8 | <15 |
| United Kingdom | 28400 | 27200 | 5 | 5 | 23 | 17 | 16 | 16 | 1.8 | 71 |
| Uruguay | 1530 | 1483 | 7 | 9 | 17 | 14 | NA | | 2.9 | 40–59 |
| USA | 122000 | 11600 | 11 | 12 | 18 | 14 | var. | | 1.8 | 79 |
| USSR | 147000 | 13100 | NA | | NA | | 18 | 18 | 2.4 | |
| Vanuatu | 52 | 59 | NA | | 4 | 5 | NA | | NA | NA |
| Venezuela | 9194 | 9192 | 8 | 9 | 5 | 5 | 16 | 16 | 4.7 | 42 |
| Vietnam | 30500 | 28900 | 42 | 39 | 7 | 6 | NA | | 5.5 | NA |
| Yemen, North | 1074 | 1051 | 33 | 30 | 5 | 4 | NA | | 6.8 | <15 |
| Yemen, South | 3448 | 3100 | 48 | 42 | 6 | 6 | 16 | 18 | 7.0 | <15 |
| Yugoslavia | 11700 | 11400 | 29 | 29 | 15 | 11 | 18 | 18 | 2.0 | 59 |
| Zaire | 16800 | 16300 | 32 | 39 | 5 | 4 | NA | | 6.1 | 1 |
| Zambia | 3354 | 3312 | 32 | 30 | 5 | 4 | 16 | 16 | 6.8 | 1 |
| Zimbabwe | 4423 | 4344 | 40 | 37 | 5 | 4 | NA | | 8.0 | 14 |

| Maternal mortality deaths per 100,000 live births | Proportion of women in labour force percentages | Labour force percentages | | Agricultural labour force percentages | | Proportion of girls in secondary education percentages | Illiteracy percentages | | Life expectancy at birth years | | Anaemia during pregnancy percentages | Right to vote won by women year |
|---|---|---|---|---|---|---|---|---|---|---|---|---|
| | | F | M | F | M | | F | M | F | M | | |
| NA | 94 | 52 | 48 | 56 | 44 | 1 | 61 | 39 | 49.2 | 45.9 | NA | 1962 |
| 85 | NA | 38 | 62 | NA | | NA | 2 | 2 | NA | | NA | 1967 |
| 48 | NA | 36 | 64 | NA | | NA | 18 | 19 | NA | | NA | 1967 |
| 85 | NA | 34 | 66 | NA | | NA | 5 | 4 | NA | | NA | 1967 |
| NA | 41 | 22 | 78 | 33 | 67 | NA | NA | | NA | | NA | NA |
| NA | 5 | 5 | 95 | 33 | 67 | 24 | 88 | 66 | 54.6 | 51.5 | NA | |
| NA | 66 | 42 | 58 | 60 | 40 | 7 | 94 | 67 | 42.9 | 39.7 | NA | 1956 |
| NA | 49 | 38 | 62 | 24 | 56 | NA | 40 | 44 | NA | | NA | NA |
| NA | 43 | 35 | 65 | 61 | 39 | 8 | 91 | 70 | 33.5 | 30.6 | 45 | 1961 |
| 11 | 38 | 35 | 65 | 23 | 77 | 58 | 26 | 8 | 73.1 | 68.6 | 26 | 1965 |
| NA | NA | NA | | NA | | NA | NA | | NA | | NA | NA |
| NA | 37 | 27 | 73 | 32 | 68 | 6 | 97 | 90 | 42.5 | 39.3 | NA | 1958 |
| 132 | 46 | 34 | 66 | 36 | 64 | 17 | NA | | 53.2 | 49.8 | 25 | |
| 16 | 34 | 25 | 75 | 26 | 74 | 86 | 11 | 5 | 76.5 | 70.6 | NA | 1931 |
| NA | 29 | 34 | 66 | 29 | 71 | 54 | 19 | 9 | 66.5 | 63.5 | 62 | 1934 |
| NA | 12 | 11 | 89 | 21 | 79 | 12 | 94 | 64 | 46.4 | 43.9 | NA | 1965 |
| NA | NA | NA | | 21 | 79 | 51 | 37 | 32 | 70.2 | 65.5 | NA | |
| NA | 71 | 46 | 54 | 49 | 51 | 40 | 47 | 43 | 49.5 | 42.9 | NA | 1968 |
| 6 | 77 | 47 | 53 | 25 | 75 | 90 | 0 | 0 | 78.3 | 72.3 | NA | 1919 |
| 9 | 50 | 36 | 64 | 26 | 74 | 57 | NA | | 78.6 | 72 | NA | 1971 |
| NA | 9 | 12 | 78 | 16 | 84 | 35 | 80 | 40 | 65.6 | 63.2 | NA | 1949 |
| NA | NA | NA | | NA | | NA | 16 | 5 | NA | | NA | |
| NA | 78 | 51 | 49 | 98 | 2 | 3 | 30 | 22 | 50.7 | 47.3 | 59 | 1961 |
| NA | 73 | 47 | 53 | 50 | 50 | 26 | 30 | 13 | 63.2 | 59.3 | 48 | 1932 |
| NA | 54 | 42 | 58 | 33 | 67 | 16 | 93 | 73 | 48.2 | 45 | 47 | 1956 |
| 17 | 33 | 29 | 71 | 22 | '78 | 57 | 10 | 5 | 71 | 66.5 | 56 | 1946 |
| NA | 7 | 23 | 77 | 21 | 79 | 23 | 75 | 49 | 58.6 | 57.6 | 38 | 1959 |
| NA | 44 | 34 | 66 | 87 | 13 | 24 | 47 | 17 | 62.8 | 58.3 | 74 | 1934 |
| NA | 46 | 34 | 66 | 35 | 65 | 3 | 60 | 35 | 51.7 | 48.3 | 35 | 1962 |
| NA | NA | NA | | 3 | 97 | 57 | 62 | 42 | 71.6 | 66.7 | NA | |
| 0 | 54 | 40 | 60 | 19 | 81 | 84 | 0 | 0 | 76 | 69.7 | NA | 1928 |
| 64 | 35 | 38 | 62 | 4 | 64 | 65 | 6 | 7 | 73 | 66.4 | NA | 1932 |
| 2 | 56 | 43 | 57 | 20 | 80 | 95 | <1 | <1 | 77.2 | 69.4 | NA | 1920 |
| NA | 58 | 51 | 49 | 44 | 56 | 121 | <1 | <1 | 74.3 | 65 | NA | 1917 |
| NA | NA | NA | | NA | | NA | NA | | NA | | NA | NA |
| 5 | 29 | 27 | 73 | 3 | 97 | 42 | 27 | 20 | 69 | 63.6 | 52 | 1947 |
| NA | 63 | 45 | 55 | 61 | 39 | 43 | NA | | 58.1 | 53.7 | NA | 1956 |
| NA | 4 | 5 | 95 | 30 | 70 | 15 | 99 | 82 | 45.1 | 43 | NA | NA |
| NA | 5 | 6 | 94 | 4 | 96 | 2 | 92 | 52 | 42.2 | 40.4 | NA | 1970 |
| 5 | 47 | 39 | 61 | 42 | 58 | 80 | 24 | 8 | 72.9 | 67.6 | NA | 1946 |
| NA | 60 | 43 | 57 | 52 | 48 | 13 | 63 | 26 | 49.7 | 46.4 | NA | 1960 |
| NA | 41 | 32 | 68 | 39 | 61 | 11 | 42 | 21 | 51 | 47.7 | 60 | 1964 |
| 6 | 36 | 29 | 71 | 26 | 74 | 13 | 39 | 24 | 55.6 | 51.3 | 27 | 1980 |

# NOTES

---

**1** ## WOMEN IN THE WORLD

This map introduces the general theme of the atlas as a whole: that while women represent more than half of the world's population, they nowhere share the same rights as men. Most of the specifics mapped in this atlas follow from this basic inequality.

The sex ratio shows the general demographic balance between men and women. It also gives information on the gendered geography of wars, migration and discrimination. Some of the countries where women greatly outnumber men reflect the loss of men in wars; others are countries with high rates of male out-migration. In the Arab Gulf states, women are greatly outnumbered by men because these countries have huge influxes of migrant male workers. But the general pattern showing where women are in the minority also reflects a more ominous influence: most of these are countries where women's status is very low. These are the countries where women work harder, die younger and die in childbirth, and where girl children are less valued.

There are many ways of summarizing women's status relative to men's. One is economic, and here the well-known United Nations quote from 1980 is still relevant: 'Women constitute half the world's population, perform nearly two-thirds of its work hours, receive one-tenth of the world's income, and own less than one-hundredth of the world's property.' Another indicator is women's legal status: nowhere in the world do women have the same legal or constitutional rights as men. The legal provision of rights does not guarantee 'equality', but it is an essential prerequisite for women's full participation in political, economic, social and cultural development – from which equality can follow.

To assess relative status among women themselves is more difficult. The status-of-women index shown on this map is meant to be used impressionistically. It elaborates on a method developed by A. Andrews (see Bibliography), whereby countries are ranked on a scale of 0 to 100, relative to the known worst case.

**Sources:** A. Andrews, 1982; IPPF, 'Women: progress towards equality', 1985; **New Internationalist**, various issues; UNIESA, **Selected Indicators**, 1985; UN World Conference for Women, **Descriptive List of National Machineries**, July 1980.

---

**2** ## YOUNG BRIDES

Millions of consensual unions lack official blessing by church and state – a fact official statistics fail to take into account. In Latin America the percentage of women in consensual unions ranges from 3 per cent in Chile, and 14 per cent in Peru, to 33 per cent in Guatemala. In Africa most women are in traditional 'marriages' governed only by local custom. In Europe and North America millions of couples 'live together'. In Sweden, for example, among people aged 20–24, 29 per cent are cohabiting while only 22 per cent are married.

National marriage laws seldom apply to everyone, especially in countries where there is great cultural diversity. Legal marriage age minimums alter according to the traditional view of the nature of male-female relations in religious or ethnic groups. Where laws *are* meant to apply universally, the reach of the law may not be long enough to touch groups in physical isolation or those with very strong traditions (as in India – see map).

Legal age minimums for marriage with parental consent range from a low of 12 (for girls) and 14 (for boys) in several Latin American countries, to a high of 22 for women and 20 for men in China. The latter statute is an integral part of China's one-child policy, probably the only country in the world with a higher marital age minimum for women than for men.

Marriage can be big business. In 1983 first-time brides and grooms in the US spent $US 20.1 billion on marriage-related goods and services; *Bride's Magazines* sells 400,000 copies every month. Although dowry has been illegal in India since 1961, a female doctor or civil servant comes with a $US 20–30,000 dowry, and the practice continues to flourish in general. Peasant girls in China fetch $US 150–300 for purchase into marriage, and bride sales are common elsewhere in the world. Arranged marriage also remains common; for example, in Anhui Province, China, it is estimated that 85 per cent are arranged; in South Korea, 40 per cent; in Sri Lanka, 50 per cent.

Marriage can lead to death. Dowry deaths (murder or suicide of a wife for insufficient dowry) are increasing in parts of India; the practice of *sati* (self-immolation or forced suicide by a widow on her husband's funeral pyre) continues.

**Sources**: Bodrova & R. Anker, 1985; J.E. Brown,1981; H. Chojnacka, 1980; IPPF, 'Youth in society', 1985; R. Morgan, 1984; K. Newland, 1979; E. Paquot 1982; J.H. Paxman, 1980; PIP, 1980, 'Age at first marriage' 1979; PRB. 'World's women', 1980; J.L. Scherer, 1983; UNIESA, **Marital Status**, 1982; US Department of Commerce, Census, **Women of the World**: Sub-Saharan Africa, 1984; WFS, 1984; WFS and ISI, 1982; **WIN News**, various issues.

## 3 DOMESTIC DISORDERS

It is hard to find information on domestic violence, which, like rape, is seriously under-reported. The information that is available hints at the magnitude of the problem: in Peru 70 per cent of all crimes reported to the police are of women being beaten by their partners; in one year (1980) in Sao Paulo, Brazil, 772 women were killed by their husbands; in Japan wife-beating has been the second-most frequent reason given for divorce initiated by women. Information on domestic violence other than wife-beating – such as incest – is not available. For wife-rape see Map 37, 'Rape'.

It is only because of the efforts of determined women in a few countries that we know as much as we do about violence in the home. Battered-women's shelters, most of which are filled to capacity all the time, only exist because of women organizing locally. It takes a huge effort to open and sustain women's shelters – often in the face of much opposition and harassment, and usually without support from local or national governments. Statistics on battered-women's shelters given on this map do NOT include various, sometimes numerous, 'hot-lines' and referral centres.

The law lags far behind these efforts. Men's violence against 'their' women and children is accepted (or ignored) across a wide spectrum of cultures. In most countries women have very little legal, or actual, protection from abusive husbands. Feminists are now pushing to have domestic violence recognized as a crime distinct from general assault laws – and for police to have powers of arrest and intervention in cases of domestic assault.

A resurgence in veiling practices is current in many Muslim countries, even where there had previously been no tradition of veiling (for example in Indonesia and Malaysia). Some Muslim women defend the veil, arguing that it is an important cultural identifier, and that it offers a degree of protection from male harassment. There is more general agreement though, that the veil is an enforced abridgement of women's rights, and exists more for men's benefit than women's. Seclusion is a related practice, whereby women are kept confined to their house or family compound. It is regarded as a symbol of a man's wealth and high status.

Domestic violence stems, in part, from the basic fact that women are widely less valued than men, girls less than boys. It is difficult to measure this imbalance. The information on son-preference shown on this map is one of the few sets of data on this topic: it shows 27 countries where parents were asked, as part of the World Fertility Survey, about their preferences for the sex of their children.

**Sources**: L. Beck & N. Keddie, 1978; Canadian Advisory Council, **Wife-Battering**, 1985; L. Lerman, 1983; Minority Rights Group, **Arab Women**, 1983; R. Morgan, 1984; press reports; B. Warrior, 1985; **WIN News**, Vol. 10, No. 4, 1984; **Women Today**, 22 March 1985.

## 4 SOCIAL SURGERY

'Social surgery' refers to operations performed for social not medical reasons. (In industrialized nations 'social surgery' includes unnecessary obstetrical, gynecological and plastic surgery – see Map 35, 'Beauty Beat'.)

It is only a decade since African women first dared to speak publicly about female circumcision, but there has been little reduction in its incidence during that time. In Sudan and Somalia, for example, infibulation (the excising of the clitoris, the labia minora and the inner walls of the labia majora, and the suturing of the two sides of the vulva), the most extreme form of circumcision, is practised on nine out of ten girls. Even though it is women who have begun to protest against the practice, it is traditionally women who perform it, and together with men, they encourage its continuation. For as long as women are dependent on marriage for survival, their sexuality will be defined by men, and they will do whatever they must to secure a husband – including mutilation and the preservation of virginity at any cost.

Doctors in Bombay's top hospitals report young upper class Arab and Muslim Indian women paying $US 1500-2000 for 'hymenoplasty', an operation restoring virginity. For all of these women, the question of sexual pleasure is moot.

Female circumcision – especially infibulation – is a major health problem in Africa and the Middle East. Thirty per cent of all Sudanese women have circumcision-related complications. During childbirth infibulated women must be opened surgically; they are sewn up again after birth. Complications can result in the death of the child or the mother. Infant mortality rates are particularly high where the incidence of circumcision is high.

The map shows the documented extent of female circumcision in Africa and the Middle East. It is also practised by Muslims in Malaysia and on the island of Java in Indonesia. According to F. Hosken the map was developed from hospital field reports, the most reliable source of information. As she points out, female circumcision is an ethnic practice and its incidence does not correspond to modern political boundaries. Calculation of the number of women and girls mutilated is based on direct information about the ethnic groups and geographic regions where genital mutilation has been confirmed by local reports. Estimates for Chad, Niger and the Central African Republic in East and Central Africa, and for Benin, Togo, Ghana and Liberia in West Africa are considered very low.

**Sources**: B. Harden, 'Africans keep rite', 13 July 1985; F. Hosken, 1980, 1982 and May/June 1982; **IPPF News**, various issues; Minority Rights Group, **Female circumcision**, 1983; E.W. Moen, 1983; E. Ogunmodede (n.d.); Population Crisis Committee, **Draper Fund Report**, 1980; D. Russell and N. Van de Ven, 1984; **WIN News**, various issues.

## 5 SINGLE STATES

The most widely available indicator of 'singleness' is the statistics on the proportion of 'women aged 45–49 never officially married'. These are the women who, in all probability, will never *be* married. Figures do exist on percentages of women who are single, but are not widely collected. The statistics that do exist obscure the fact that women who are in consensual unions (married without benefit of official sanction) are counted – officially – as single. On the other hand, some women do not wish to be identified as single (marriage confers status – see text for Map 2, 'Young Brides'), and so do not reveal their true situation to census takers.

The right to divorce is important for women. Often, however, it means a precipitous drop in an ex-wife's (and usually her children's) standard of living. In the US it is estimated that divorce results in an average decrease of 42 per cent in a woman's income and an *increase* of 73 per cent in a man's.

Divorce rate statistics do not take into account both legal (for example, separation) and illegal (for example, abandonment) marital dissolution other than divorce. Though incomplete, figures do reflect the relative ease or difficulty of obtaining a divorce, including the ability to pay for one, as well as the authority of the prevailing religious system. Catholic countries which have only recently legalized divorce have low rates (for example, Italy). In Muslim countries also divorce is relatively rare; polygyny and social disapproval appear to lower men's need for divorce, while for women it is hardly an option. 'Talaq' – the Muslim practice of simply declaring intent to divorce – is a male prerogative.

In many countries poverty and social stigmatization leave divorced and widowed women in a very precarious social position. (Widows are not even allowed to remarry in some countries.) The 'confirmed bachelor' is a more accepted station than 'spinsterhood'.

**Sources:** Christian Science Monitor, 24 July 1984; G. Kurian, 1984; PIP, 'Laws and policies', 1984; UN, Demographic Yearbook, 1982; UNIESA, **Marital Status, Summary Report**, 1982, and Marital Status, Comparative Analysis, 1983; US Department of Commerce, Census, **Women of the World: Near East and North Africa**, 1985, Asia and the Pacific, 1985, Sub-Saharan Africa, 1984; J. W. Wilkie, 1980; WIN News, various issues.

## 6 MOTHERS

One of the biggest differences between the rich and the poor world lies in the number of children that women have. (This is officially called the 'total fertility rate', and is defined as 'the average number of children that would be born to a woman if she lived through her childbearing years and bore children at the prevailing age-specific rates.) In Western Europe fertility rates are the lowest in the world – and in some cases have dropped below population replacement rates, much to the alarm of many government and military planners. Women in sub-Saharan Africa and the Arab states have the world's highest fertility rates.

The world's 'population problem', therefore, is conventionally defined as a problem of certain countries – and of certain women. But high fertility rates are the consequence of many factors. It is closely related to age at marriage; where early marriage for girls is encouraged (see Map 2, 'Young Brides'), women will spend a longer part of their lives in childbearing, and will have more children. As it stands, the interval between the first and last birth for women in Kenya is almost 19 years; in Jordan, 18 years; in Syria and Mexico, 17 years – compared with 7 years in the United States. Fertility is linked to knowledge of and access to contraceptives – which is usually a function of state policy (see Map 7, 'Population Policies' and Notes). Many population programmes are designed only to persuade women to use contraceptives, not to educate them about contraception – resulting in a high failure rate. High fertility is linked to poverty and its related high infant mortality rates: to end up with a family of four or five, a woman may bear ten children. In poorer and agricultural economies children are an economic asset. In many countries a woman's status goes with the number of children she bears. More to the point, in many countries men feel that their 'manhood' is proved by the number of children they can father.

Infertility is less well documented, but affects a significant proportion of women around the world; the average infertility rate in sub-Saharan Africa is 12 per cent. Since women's status is often determined by their ability to bear children, infertility can be a particular hardship – and often a serious threat to health. Where a couple cannot have children, the problem is almost invariably put down to the woman's infertility.

New reproductive technologies are being developed, ostensibly to help women with reproductive difficulties. In fact, the benefits are available to only a few, and the structure of these new reproductive technologies is such that women's control over the reproductive process is jeopardized; women become the providers of the raw materials (eggs, ovaries) for an industrial process of reproduction that is largely controlled by the male doctors and technicians developing the technologies.

**Sources**: Council of Europe, **Family Formation**, 1982; K.T. de Graft-Johnson, 1980; G. Kurian, 1984; PRB, '1984 World population data sheet'; UN, **Demographic Yearbook**, 1981, 1983, 1984; UN Decade for Women, **Selected Statistics**, 1985; UN Fund for Population Activities Compendium (yearly); UNIESA, **The World Population Situation in 1983**, 1984; US Department of Commerce, **Women of the World: Sub-Saharan Africa**, 1984; Women's Emergency Conference, 1985; World Bank, **World Development Report, 1984**.

## 7 POPULATION POLICIES

The population policies of most governments are difficult to interpret. Only a few governments have clearly defined and explicit policies. The one-child policy of China is well known, and is one of the most explicit population policies in the world. Romania currently has one of the most repressive – and also explicit – policies, limiting women's access to contraceptives and family planning services (see Notes to Map 9, 'Abortion').

Pro-natalist governments want women to have more children, usually to bolster military strength. Some governments, such as France, East Germany and Finland have official pro-natalism stances, but they do not enforce it. Other governments, such as Kuwait, Chad and Laos go to great lengths to bolster pro-natalism – by outlawing contraceptives, clamping down on abortions, and offering hefty incentives to women to have large numbers of children. At its worst, pro-natalism can effectively mean forced breeding for women.

The majority of the world's governments have policies designed to reduce or stabilize the population, and most support family planning to some extent. 'Strong' government support for family planning usually means that the government sponsors educational programmes, supports clinics, distributes contraceptives and offers incentives to women to have fewer children. In 'direct support' countries, governments may subsidize family planning clinics or encourage educational programmes, but involvement ranges from being systematic to being quite casual. 'Indirect support' usually means simply that the government allows private family planning agencies to operate – or otherwise does not erect legislative barriers.

Like pro-natalism, population *reduction* policies can slip over into coercion. Sterilization abuse (which includes forced sterilization and sterilization without informed consent) is widespread, though can only be documented for a handful of countries. Other forms of reproductive abuses – for example the charges of forced abortions in China – are almost impossible to document. We make no attempt to map them here, but *do* note that they exist.

National government population policy is often influenced by and dependent upon international aid. With the exception of India and China (which mainly finance their own population programmes), foreign aid pays for an average of 50 per cent of all population programmes in poorer countries. International population aid is generally beneficial to women – and, in fact, more of it is needed since millions of women in the world have no access to family planning services. But dependency on foreign aid leaves women vulnerable to policies and decisions made well beyond their country and beyond their reach. Family planning aid becomes a political tool – it may be withdrawn, increased or decreased for reasons that have nothing to do with women's health or their reproductive choices. This is most clearly illustrated by the current shift in US government policies that are jeopardizing the ability of women the world over to make reproductive choices. The US government is imposing an anti-abortion morality on all funding decisions, and has withdrawn support from major population agencies (including the International Federation for Planned Parenthood and the UN Fund for Population Activities) because these agencies do not condemn abortion. Family planning for millions of women hangs in the balance.

**Sources**: Boston Women's Health Book Collective (file materials); **Family Planning in the 1980s**; PIP, 'Laws and policies' 1984; PRB, 'Family planning', 1981; UN, **World Population Trends**, 1981 and 1983; UN Fund for Population Activities; UNIESA **The World Population Situation**, 1984; World Bank, **World Development Report 1984**.

## 8 CONTRACEPTION

Women the world over face the dilemma that 'effective contraceptives tend to be unsafe, and safe contraceptives tend not to be effective'. For many women contraceptives are not available at all. Making contraceptives and making them available to women rests in the hands of governments, pharmaceutical manufacturers, and international aid agencies – all of which may be working at odds with one another, and with the women for whom the contraceptives are intended. Women's voices and women's needs often get lost in the labyrinth of big business, big bureaucracy, and international policy-making.

Virtually all contraceptives manufacturers are subsidiaries of large multinational pharmaceutical firms. The world market is dominated by five companies: Wyeth Labs (USA), Ortho Pharmaceuticals (USA), G.D. Searle (USA), Syntex (USA), and Schering AG (West Germany). The most profitable contraceptive is 'the Pill', an estimated 54 million women worldwide are on it. But new products are constantly being tested – often by the dubious means of trying it out on women in poor countries before marketing it in industrial nations. The current controversy over the new injectable contraceptive, 'DepoProvera', is due in part to this sort of testing programme. Lawsuits and public outcry over the DepoProvera case and the faulty and dangerous IUD, the 'Dalkon Shield', have prompted the major manufacturers to retreat from product development and testing. There are few developments in male contraceptives since neither private nor public research money is directed toward it.

In Third World countries most contraceptives are distributed through the public sector. Governments and family planning agencies buy contraceptives from the pharmaceutical companies and distribute them free or at cost. The major world suppliers of contraceptive aid are: Agency for International Development (AID), the UN Fund for Population Activities, Swedish International Development Authority (SIDA), and International Planned Parenthood Federation (IPPF). Millions of women are dependent on these four for contraceptives supply – which also means that these women are vulnerable to policy changes made thousands of miles away, shifts in funding priorities, or shifting political favours.

**Sources**: Drug Store News, various issues; D.L. Nortman, 1982; E. Paquot, 1982; PIP, 'Oral contraceptives', 1982; PRB, 'Fertility and status', 1981; UN, **World Population Trends**, 1981 and 1983; S. Urang, 1983; US Congress, Office of Technology Assessment Technologies, 1982; World Bank, **World Development Report**, 1984; World Pharmaceutical News, **Scrip**, 1981–84.

## 9 ABORTION

Thirty to fifty-five million abortions occur annually, about half of which are illegal, and half of which take place in poor countries.

Most abortions are undergone by married, older women with completed families. In the West and in urban Africa it is mostly younger, unmarried women who have abortions in order to postpone childbearing. The main reasons for women choosing abortion are lack of or failure of contraception, a change in personal circumstances (for example, desertion, widowhood, financial problems), or detection of birth defects. (In India amniocentesis – originally developed to detect fetal abnormalities – is increasingly being used to establish fetal gender, followed by abortion of females.)

In poor countries illegal abortion kills 50–1000 women per 100,000 procedures. It is 10–250 times more dangerous to have an abortion there as it is to use *any* form of birth control. Up to 70 per cent of maternal deaths are due to complications following illegal abortion. Legalization of abortion reduces maternal mortality, especially where abortions are also affordable and widely available (legalization does not guarantee access).

Some religions tolerate abortion, some do not. Where church and state are intertwined, abortion laws follow religious dictates, as in Muslim and some Catholic countries. Government population policy can also determine abortion law: on International Women's Day in 1984, Romanian President Ceausescu declared that 'it is every healthy Romanian woman's duty to have four children'. In an attempt to increase the labour force, stringent anti-abortion laws were suddenly brought in. Monthly gynaecological checks for women in the state's industrial complexes were instituted to insure that no woman had a (now-illegal) abortion. On the other hand, the perceived need to reduce population in Singapore and Tunisia resulted in liberalized laws. In Cyprus abortion following rape was legalized after that country's civil war; war-time rape of women by soldiers necessitated the change. Doctors and midwives making a good living off illegal abortion effectively oppose abortion and contraception availability in some countries in the Middle East and South East Asia.

Reliable data on abortion is hard to come by. Reported, legal abortions are often a fraction of the true abortion rate; and there is no reliable data on the incidence of illegal abortion – only best guesses.

**Sources**: R. Cook, et al., 1977; George Washington University, 'Pregnancy termination', 1973 and 'Law and policy', 1976; International Reference Center, **Abortion Research Notes**, 1983, 1984; G. Kurian, 1984; E.G. Moore-Cavar, 1974;
R. Morgan, 1984; Population Council, 1984; Populatin Crisis Committee, '**Improving the Status of women**, 1980 and **Population**, 1982; Population Institute, 1984; F. Sanchez-Torres, 1980; C. Tietze, 1983; UN, Demographic Yearbook, 1981, 1982; P. Wise, 1984; A. Wolfson, 1983.

One-quarter of all deaths in the world occur among children under five, two-thirds of whom are infants. Ninety-seven per cent of infant deaths happen in developing countries. Three million infants die each year in India alone; another two million in Bangladesh, Nigeria, Indonesia and Pakistan combined.

Infant mortality rates could be dramatically lowered through primary health care (see Notes to Map 26, 'Illness and Health') providing midwifery, encouragement to breastfeed, vaccinations, ORT (oral-rehydration therapy against diarrhoea), and antibiotics against infection.

Changes in women's social condition would also make a difference. Girls and women in school delay childbearing. This results in both lowered infant (and maternal) mortality rates and educated mothers with greater opportunities in life. High infant mortality itself encourages high birth rates – to replace children who have died. When infant mortality rates drop, fewer and healthier children are born.

The infant mortality rate statistics used here represent five-year averages to avoid using occasionally skewed single-year figures. The USSR rate is considered very conservative; it is known to be rising as a result of annual flu epidemics, increasing alcoholism, poor prenatal care, high abortion rates and declining breastfeeding. Official statistics have been unavailable since 1974.

Abortion is a leading cause of maternal mortality in some countries. Where abortion is legal abortion rates do not necessarily decline, but maternal deaths from abortion do. In Latin America abortion accounts for 30–50 per cent of all maternal deaths; it is the leading cause in Caracas, according to estimates. In India one woman dies from a septic abortion every ten minutes.

Maternal mortality is an important index of a community's commitment to women's health care. Maternal-related deaths are among the leading causes of death for women aged 15–44 in poor countries. It is the leading or second-leading cause of death in one-third of these countries. Adequate prenatal and birth care could prevent most of those deaths resulting from toxaemia, haemorrhage, sepsis, anaemia, obstructed labour and other complications. Teenage women having too many babies too quickly, who are inadequately nourished and rested, face an unacceptable high risk of death in childbirth.

Maternal mortality statistics are often not collected, or if collected are not reported (for example in the USSR, mentioned above), especially where rates are known to be high. Where rates *are* reported, they are often under-reported. In countries with well-developed health care systems and well-documented statistics, rates average 5–30 deaths per 100,000 live births. In parts of Africa rates of 1000 per 100,000 live births have been reported. Everywhere rates are higher for poor and minority women.

**Sources**: W.U. Chandler, 1984; M. Feshbach, 1982; Pakistan, Ministry of Information and Broadcasting, **Women in Pakistan** (n.d.); P. Huston, 1978; M. Islam, 1977; R. Morgan, 1984; K. Newland, 1981; PAHO, 1982; C. Tietze, 1977; UN, **Demographic Yearbook**, 1982; UN World Conference for Women, **Statistical Abstract**, 1980; UNICEF, **State of World's Children**, **1984** and **1985**, and **Assignment Children**, 1980; US Department of Commerce, Census, **Women in the World: Latin American and the Caribbean**, 1984; WHO, **Sixth Report**, 1980; Women for Women, 1977; World Bank, **Development Report 1984**.

'Midwife' is an umbrella term that actually includes two different types of birth attendants: a) 'traditional birth attendants', usually rural women, midwives by practice and by tradition, but without medical training; b) 'midwife', usually women with some medical training, and often with some sort of accreditation.

The percentage of births attended by trained personnel (doctors, nurses, trained midwives) varies considerably according to region. In Africa only 34 per cent of all births are attended by a medically-trained attendant; in Asia the figure is 49 per cent; in Latin America, 64 per cent; in Europe, 97 per cent; and in North America, 100 per cent. These figures reflect the role of traditional birth attendants in providing maternity support to the world's women. The World Health Organization estimates that 45 per cent of all babies in the world are delivered by traditional birth attendants. Midwives and traditional birth attendants (the overwhelming majority of whom are women) together deliver about 80 per cent of all babies in the Third World.

The aim of most governments is to turn their traditional birth attendants into midwives. To this end, traditional birth attendants have been outlawed in a number of countries, including Egypt, Lebanon, and the Sudan. Until recently, midwives were outlawed in North America. Over the past century the powerful medical establishment there went to great lengths to eradicate midwives; doctors saw midwives as competition and as a threat to their monopoly on medical knowledge. Midwifery survived, though, and is now enjoying a comeback in most industrial countries.

**Sources**: Council of Europe, 1975; D.L. Nortman, 1982; M. Owen, 1983; PIP, 'Traditional midwives and family planning', 1980; **Statistical Yearbook for Asia and the Pacific**, 1982; UN Decade for Women, **Selected Statistics**, 1985; UNICEF, **State of World's Children 1985**; WHO, **Coverage of Maternity Care**, 1985, **Health and Status of Women**, 1980, and **World Health Statistics**, 1983.

## 12 FAMILIES

Conventional definitions of 'family' revolve around the presence of children. Because women everywhere have primary responsibility for childcare, 'the family' for them is as much a work unit as an emotional one. But the workload on women varies widely. This is suggested by the dependency ratio presented on the main map: the ratio of pre-school children (under age five) to women. Higher dependency ratios mean that direct childcare demands (feeding, health care, etc.) are greater, and indirect demands, such as agricultural labour, and water and firewood collecting are also greater.

The demands of childcare are what keep women most confined to the home, and keep them out of the waged workforce. Out-of-the-home childcare is radically short of the need for it, worldwide. Only the Scandinavian and Eastern European governments recognize childcare as a legitimate public policy responsibility. Elsewhere women must either patch together whatever help they can find (usually relying on older family members) or pay a large share of their income on private childcare (a growing problem now in the USA). As more and more women form single-parent households (see Map 28, 'Poverty') through divorce or choice, the childcare crisis will grow.

Global trends indicate that the nuclear family is slowly replacing the extended family as the standard household configuration. Consequently household sizes are shrinking. The smallest households are found in Europe; the largest in the Arab states. Twelve countries report an average household size of over six people: Afghanistan, Algeria, Bahrain, Botswana, Fiji, Kenya, Kiribati, Kuwait, Maldives, Nicaragua, Surinam, and Syria.

With the notable exception of North America it is unusual – and often unacceptable – for anyone, but especially women, to live alone – women's lives in most places are lived entirely in the context of a family. Although it is women's role as mothers that appears to give 'families' their raison d'etre, control of the family usually runs through the men involved. Women live in the house and in the family of their father/husband/brother. In this way the family forms the primary unit of social control, particularly over women. It is for this reason that many feminists argue that social change for women must start with the family – and the conclusion that 'the personal is political' derives largely from this sort of analysis.

**Sources**: V. Bodrova, & R. Anker, 1985; G. Kurian, 1984; C. Lemke, 1985; New Internationalist, Dec 1982; PRB, 'Changing American family', 1983; Statistics Sweden, 1985; UN Decade for Women, **Selected Statistics**, 1985; UN, **Demographic Yearbook**, 1981 and 1982; UNECA, **Demographic Data Sheets**, 1983, and **Day Care**,1981; UN World Conference for Women, **Statistical Abstract**, 1980.

## 13 TIME BUDGETS

The unequal division of labour is universal. Our most deeply ingrained assumptions about a woman's proper place – in the home and taking care of children – determine the way women spend their time. In poor and rich countries alike it is women – with a few exceptions – who do the subsistence work: feeding, clothing, tending and tilling – in short, managing their families' survival. And very few women see themselves as 'just housewives'; in Tamil Nadu, India, for example, poor women see their role as 'earning for and supporting the family'.

All over the globe there is still 'women's work' and 'men's work'; but the traditional divisions of labour by sex are breaking down – on women's side. In rich countries, where women are increasingly part of the workforce, they do a double shift: in the office or factory by day and then at domestic chores by night. In Italy, 85 per cent of husbands do no housework; in the UK 72 per cent of housework is done 'mostly by women'. In the US more than half of the female labour force is married and the biggest increase in employment has been among women with pre-school children. This results not only in overwork but also in handicapped job prospects: a young mother cannot work overtime, travel or be flexible enough for company promotions.

In poor countries traditional family structures are breaking down as men are drawn to the cities and into the cash economy. Yet for women 'economic development' often means more work and less control of resources. Husbands are less likely to help out as they are freed from traditional male domestic responsibilities – but women are expected to assist in their husband's cash crop production in addition to maintaining their own family plots. Training for double-duty begins early, as children imitate their parents. In Zaire, for example, girls do 55 per cent as much work around the house as their mothers, boys only 15 per cent.

The value of women's unpaid labour is estimated at 25–40 per cent of measured GNP in industrialized countries. Another estimate values it as adding one-third – or $US 4000 billion – to the world's economic product.

'Equal opportunity' and 'economic development' must not merely translate into an opportunity for women to work more and control less. The greatest injustice is perhaps to be found as much in inequality in the home as in the workplace.

Information for this spread mostly comes from individual researchers' field data, sometimes published by the international development agencies or the UN. Governments in the West are just beginning to sponsor collection of time-use data; until recently what went on behind closed doors held no interest for official statisticians.

**Sources**: M. Acharya et al., 1979; Austrian Federal Ministry of Social Affairs (n.d); L. Beneria, 1984; V. Bodrova & R. Anker, 1985; J.E. Brown, 1981; B.M. Buvinic et al., 1978; CEC, **European Women and Men**, 1978; Consumers Association of Penang, 1982; R. Dixon, 1978; FAO, 1983; L. Goldschmidt-Clermont, 1983; ILO, **Womanpower**, 1975; ISIS, 'Motherhood', 1982; G. Lapidus, 1978; **New Internationalist**, July 1985; K. Newland, 1980; OECD, 1975; D. Ramprakash, 1986; A.K.N. Reddy, 1980; B. Rogers, 1980; R. L. Sivard, 1985; Social and Cultural Planning, Netherlands, 1985; Statistics Sweden, 1985; UNECA, **Critical Needs**, 1981, **Integration of Women**, 1974, and **Women of Africa**, 1975; UNICEF, **Assignment Children**, 1980, and **Situation of Women in Kenya**, 1985; World Bank, **World Development Report 1984**.

## 14 AGRICULTURE

Women produce most of the food for home comsumption and are an important part of the paid agricultural labour force. They harvest coffee in Rwanda, pick bananas and pineapples in Martinique and tea in Sri Lanka and farm shrimp in coastal India. They are also active as traders and marketers. In Ghana, over 87 per cent of traders are women. Women also keep small animals for sale at market and use at home. Women's agricultural labour is not normally given much consideration in agricultural development schemes or in education, training, financial credit and extension programmes. Yet it is women who make many of the most critical agricultural decisions, from which seed to plant to when and how to harvest.

In Africa, only five per cent of all trained agricultural personnel are female. In 13 African countries they make up less than one per cent, and in only four countries are they over ten per cent. Women represent approximately half of all agricultural students in the USSR and Romania; in the UK and Australia, around 15 per cent and in Ecuador and Swaziland, fewer than five per cent. In Africa, technical and credit assistance for women, such as it is, is concentrated in home economics (where 100 per cent of students are female).

Modernization of agriculture often means mechanization of production and land 'reform'. The new (high) technology lightens men's workloads because it is used to help produce cash crops and shift male work patterns away from home. Women's work increases because of the loss of male help in subsistence farming and the loss of control over any crops which may have started to procure money. Land 'reform' often means a shift from traditional (often communal or even matrilineal) to private and/or patrilineal land ownership, denying women access to land they have long farmed for their families and to any cash it might generate.

In the USA the role of farmers' wives in farm management and agricultural production is often overlooked. Women in the USA only *own* five per cent of all farms, though this is a two-fold increase over the past decade.

**Sources**: G. Ashworth, 'Daughters', (n.d); K. Cloud, 1977; C. D. Deere and M. Léon de Leal, 1982; **Demography** (monthly); FAO, **Information Note**, 1983; E. Hong, 1983; ILO, **Yearbook 1982**; ISIS, 'Women, land and food', 1979; M. McAndrew and J. Peers, (n.d.); R. Morgan, 1984; **New York Times**, 15 October 1984; PRB, **World's Women Data Sheet** 1980; Rogers, 1979; Safilios-Rothschild, **Conventional Indicators**, 1983; UN Decade for Women, **(K) Rural Development**, 1984 and **Selected Statistics**, 1985; UNESCAP, 'Reflections of decade'; UNESCO, **Yearbook**, 1982; UN World Conference for Women, **Women in Rural Areas**, 1980; US Department of Commerce, Census, **Women of the World: Asia and the Pacific**, 1985, **Near East and North Africa**, 1985, **Latin America and the Caribbean**, 1984, and **Sub-Saharan Africa**, 1984; World Bank, **World Development Report 1984**.

## 15 LABOUR FORCE

Official statistics on women in the labour force are the only broad-based economic indicators according to sex available internationally. But there are serious flaws in the definitions of 'work', 'labour force', and 'economic activity' – flaws that tend to mean that much of women's work is overlooked. Further, the quality of data and the definitions used vary from country to country. So, while the general impression of labour force activity worldwide is fairly reliably portrayed, the figures are not sufficiently accurate to support elaborate interpretations. Since the International Labour Organization (ILO) is virtually the only agency that collects and compiles international labour force data, it is not possible to confirm, compare, or criticise their figures using alternative sources. The ILO has consistently made an effort to collect and report data by sex – and they have done better at this than almost any other of the large international agencies.

Labour force statistics generally include only formally structured waged work – work, for example, for which there is official employee registration. Much of women's work falls beyond these boundaries. Millions of women work in the informal sector (as domestic servants or market traders, for example) and this labour goes uncounted. At the far end of the work continuum is all of the unpaid labour done by women; Maps 13, 'Time Budgets', and 14, 'Agriculture', deal with this phenomenon and help to provide a more balanced view of the world's work done by women.

The reported decrease over time in African women's labour force participation is most likely due to methods of counting and compiling labour statistics. The decrease in the USSR is more likely explained by shifts in the demographic balance between women and men since the end of World War Two.

Sources: A. Cropper, 1980; ILO, Women at Work, various issues, World Labour Report, 1985, and Yearbook, 1984; R. Morgan, 1984; R. L. Sivard, 1985; UN Decade for Women, (A) Employment, 1984, and Selected Statistics, 1985; WIN News, Spring 1984.

## 16 OUT TO WORK

One of the biggest worldwide economic shifts this century is the entry of women into the paid labour market. Some women have always worked for wages; the big change is that now women of all classes and ages work. However, it is still much more true for women than men that participation in the labour force is influenced by such factors as marital status, age and family responsibilities. Marriage and childbearing are the two most important influences that keep women out of the waged workforce. In a number of countries (amoung them, Lichtenstein, Rwanda, Burundi, Swaziland, and the Philippines) husbands have the legal right to restrict their wives' choice to work outside the home and, in some cases, to prohibit it altogether. Many employers discriminate against hiring married women, whether or not this is within the law.

Women's wages are vital to their own survival and that of their families. This is clearly the case in single-parent families. A 1984 study in the UK showed that homes with married women working are 35 per cent better off than homes without. Other studies show that women spend a greater proportion of their income than men on family necessities such as food and shelter.

While more and more women go out to work, most social structures and government policies are constructed as though the stay-at-home wife was the norm. The lack of childcare facilities (see Map 12, 'Families') is the most striking indication of this conflict.

The cautions about data in the notes for Map 15, 'Labour Force', generally apply to the data on this map too.

Sources: CEC, Supplement 15, 1984; ILO, Women at Work, No. 2, 1982, World Labour Report, 1985, and Yearbook, 1982, 1983 and 1984; M. Mukhopadhyay, 1984; R.L. Sivard, 1985; UN Decade for Women, (A) Employment, 1984; US Department of Labor, Handbook, 1983; WIN News, various issues; Women of Europe, Jan 1985.

## 17 MIGRANT WORKERS

Migration is usually treated as though it were a predominantly male experience. In fact, women are an important and growing proportion of the world's migrants, and some migrant streams consist almost entirely of women. A 1985 study by the US Department of Labor showed that 66 per cent of all immigrants to the United States are now women – a rise from 41 per cent at the turn of the century.

The patterns of women's migration, and of work in the host country, are distinctive. Women who move to cities from rural areas typically face severe discrimination, and end up being employed in the worst paid and least regulated work sectors. Domestic service and the garment industry are, universally, job ghettoes for migrant women. Prostitution is often taken up as a last resort. Women's migration is closely linked to the growing feminization of poverty, the increasing feminization of agriculture, and increasing prostitute exploitation (see related Maps 28, 'Poverty', and 36, 'Sex for Sale').

The line between voluntary and forced migrations is sometimes very thin. Migrants who are fleeing harsh economic conditions are often no better off than refugees. Governments occasionally encourage migration as part of a planned economic programme: overseas workers can be a major source of foreign currency, and migration can alleviate labour problems at home. Women's lives are affected by migration even when they themselves do not move. Male migration is an important factor in increasing rural female poverty and in the increase in women-headed households.

Some migration patterns change rapidly, and international reporting cannot keep pace. Statistics on migrants, therefore, should be used with caution, and may indicate migrant streams that are no longer current.

Sources: The Economist, 3 December 1983; ILO, World Labour Report, 1985; Inside Asia, Nov/Dec 1984; ISIS 'Migrant women', 1980; Migration Today, No.s 30 & 31, 1983, No. 33, 1984; Minority Rights Group, Western Europe's Migrant Workers, 1982; A. Phizacklea, 1983; Population Crisis Committee, 'World population growth', 1983; UN Decade for Women, (A) Employment, 1984; USAID, Women in International Migration, 1980.

## 18 JOB GHETTOS

The map depicting job ghettos around the world does NOT show 'the jobs where most women work'; it shows the jobs where most of the workers are women – it shows the jobs that are typically feminized. We are not suggesting, for example, that most women who work in the UK work at office cleaning, but we are saying that most office cleaners are women.

There is a marked worldwide division into 'women's' and 'men's' jobs, but the set of women's jobs is not the same in every country. 'Women's work' in Sri Lanka is tea picking; in Nigeria it is market trading; in the USA it is nursing, childcare, primary school teaching, for example. 'Women's work' is usually considered undignified for men to do, and in any event it is usually too poorly paid and menial to attract competition from male workers. Men's jobs, on the other hand, are often well-paid and highly respected, and women have a very hard time breaking into their ranks.

The increasingly internationalized industrial production system in textiles and electronics has created a widespread common job ghetto: women electronics workers in the USA and in Singapore.often work for the same employer. The creation of these female job ghettos is often an integral part of government economic planning. Many governments in South East Asia, for example, actively try to attract foreign investment by promising a docile, willing, hard working labour pool of young women.

**Sources**: V. Bodrova & R. Anker, 1985; W. Chapkis & C. Enloe, 1983; A. Fuentes & B. Ehrenreich, 1983; M. Gill & J. Massiah, 1984; ILO, **Problems of women non-manual workers**, 1981, and **Yearbook**, 1984; R. Morgan, 1984; S. Quinn-Judge, 1983; UNECA, **Mozambique**, 1980; UNESCAP, **Social Development Newsletter**, No. 10, 1984; US Department of Labor, **Time of Change**, 1984; **WIN News**, various issues.

## 19 EARNINGS

Women's experience of the workplace is different from men's. The earnings gap is among those differences – and derives from a set of interconnections that describe many women's working conditions. Women's low wages result in part from their ghettoization in certain jobs, the fact that most part-time work is done by women, and the lack of job training provided by menial and part-time work. In turn, low wages prevent women from 'getting ahead' and escaping their restrictive job choices.

An increasing proportion of all people who are 'poor' are the wage-earning poor: people who work, but whose wages fall below minimum needs. Women are a large proportion of this new class. Since pensions and other benefits are usually based on earnings, women's low earning at work has ripple effects throughout their lives.

Figures on wage comparison represent the total wage *earnings* of women and men – that is, what the average woman and man bring home as a pay packet at the end of a day, week or year. They do not necessarily represent wage per hour (or wage per week) comparisons.

The job categories used for specific wage comparisons include a wide range. 'Professional and technical workers' include librarians, lawyers, doctors, nurses, writers, engineers, teachers. 'Managers and administrators' include sales managers and all administrators in both private and public sector jobs. 'Craft workers' mostly consist of bakers, brick masons, carpenters, machinists, and electricians.

Part-time work is a mixed blessing for women: it offers a way for them to combine waged work with domestic responsibilities, but it leaves them economically marginalized. Women who work part-time are more ghettoized into low-esteem, low-paying jobs than women working full-time. Part-time workers usually receive no benefits, pension coverage or union protection. Because women are encouraged to work part-time – to be exploited workers *and* 'superwomen' – men are allowed to continue avoiding family and household responsibilities. The fact that part-time work is mainly a female phenomenon reflects, in part, the attitudes of men to family responsibilities. Of all part-time workers in the UK, 94 per cent are women; in West Germany, also 94 per cent; in Sweden, 85 per cent; in Australia, 79 per cent; in the USA, 70 per cent. In 1984 the Iranian government legislated that women who work in offices or factories can work *only* half-time – on the basis that women's work is not very valuable in the first place, and that women should properly be devoting most of their time to being wives and mothers.

**Sources**: CEC, **Supplement 10**, 1982; Eurostat, 1980; ILO, **Chart**, 1984, **Problems of Women Non-Manual Workers**, 1981, and **Women at Work**, various issues; A. McAuley, 1981; R. Morgan, 1984; press reports; N. Rytina, 1982; R.L. Sivard, 1985; UNESCO, **Yearbook**, 1981; UN Decade for Women, **(A) Employment**, 1984; **WIN News**, various issues.

## 20 JOB PROTECTION

Women are more likely than men to become unemployed, especially when jobs are scarce – so, 'hard times' often hit women hardest of all. 'Youth unemployment' is usually portrayed as mostly a male problem, but in fact it is as much, or more, of a problem for women:

**Unemployment rates for people under age 25, 1981, USA** percentages

|  | Men | Women |
| --- | --- | --- |
| Whites | 13.7 | 11.7 |
| Blacks | 30.6 | 31.7 |
| Hispanics | 17.0 | 17.8 |

The prevailing attitude that work is less serious and less important for women than for men, often means that women's unemployment is treated as a trivial concern. But with more and more families worldwide relying wholly or partly on women's wages, unemployment is a major problem – and , in turn, fuels the growing feminization of poverty (see Map 28, 'Poverty').

As a general rule, official records of unemployment undercount the unemployed – and never take into account the 'underemployed' (people who are working a part-time or poorly paid job simply because no appropriate job exists): this means that women's actual unemployment could be as much as two-times higher than reported.

Maternity often brings unemployment for women. There are *very* few safeguards to protect women's right to a job – and to maternity leave – during and after pregnancy. In many countries the maternity leave policies on the books remain unenforced and have little effect on private employers who routinely fire or 'ease out' pregnant workers. The USA stands worst among industrial nations in providing maternity protection – the only protection that women in the USA have is whatever they can work out privately with their employer. Maternity leave has yet to be taken seriously as a public policy issue.

Women at work tend to be much less unionized than men – in part because many women work in socially-isolated, hard-to-organize jobs: domestic service, or home-work piece-assembly, for example. Sometimes men, fearing competition, act to block women's entry to unionized labour. The end result is that women's rate of participation in unions lags far behind their participation in the labour market. Furthermore, with the exception of Eastern European countries, women have little voice in union power structures.

**Sources**: CEC, Supplement No. 9, 1982, and **Supplement No. 10**, 1982; European Documentation, 1984; ILO, **Women at Work**, No. 2, 1982, and No. 2, 1984, **World Labor Report**, 1985 and **Yearbook**, 1984; R. Morgan, 1984; R.L. Sivard, 1985; UN World Conference for Women, **Report**, 1980; US Department of Labor, **Time of Change**, 1984.

## 21 ACCESS TO MEANS

It is difficult to make cross-cultural comparisons of women's land rights. There is no international survey of these rights, and there is often little uniformity within a single country: women's land rights may vary according to local tribal, religious, or customary laws. On related topics, such as women's access to credit, there is no international data at all.

The status of women with regard to property is closely related to the concept 'head of household' – the head of household is generally accorded authority over joint property. If men are automatically assumed to be the household head, then in the normal state of affairs it is assumed that men will control all property, even property jointly acquired.

In most countries men still have the right to determine choice of married domicile. For most women this means that when they get married they leave their home and family to join the household of their husband. In doing this they forfeit any property rights they may have held in their name. For many women in the world, becoming married also means becoming landless. In countries where women have an equal right to choose the married domicile, this is a very recent change: almost nowhere did women have this right before the 1970s. In Switzerland women only won this right in 1983. The idea that women should be entitled to a share of their husband's wealth acquired during marriage is an even more recent and more radical legal departure – and in most countries women do not have this protection.

In general women worldwide have access to wealth and resources primarily through their husbands or fathers – they do not have independent means. International aid is also generally directed to, and by, men. Two international organizations are working to change this: Women's World Banking is an international banking organization offering loans to Third World women; the UN Voluntary Fund for Women raises money for development projects for women.

**Sources**: FAO, 1979; C. Heckathorn, 1980; R. Hirschon, 1984; A.E. Mayer; R. Morgan, 1984; B. Rogers, 1979; UN Decade for Women, **World Survey on the Role of Women in Development**, 1984; **WIN News**, Summer 1984; **Women of Europe**, various issues.

## 22 SCHOOL DAYS

Girls' access to basic education has improved greatly over the past two decades. There was an 'enrolment boom' in the 1960s and 1970s that pushed girls into the classroom as never before. But inequities still exist: boys are more educated than girls, and girls in rich countries and in cities are more educated than those in poor countries or rural settings.

In Burkina Faso, Ethiopia, Bhutan, Afghanistan and Papua New Guinea, among others, fewer than 10 per cent of primary age girls were in school in 1960. In 1980 percentages ranged from a virtually unchanged 11 per cent in Afghanistan to an impressive 54 per cent in Papua New Guinea. By contrast, in countries as diverse as Guyana, Portugal, the USSR, Kuwait and New Zealand, virtually all eligible girls attended primary school then as they do now. In cities all over the globe, more girls go to school than do their rural counterparts; in Burundi, 60 per cent of eligible urban girls attend school compared with 7 per cent of rural girls; in Guatemala the ratio is 66 per cent to 30 per cent; in Nepal it is 36 per cent to 4 per cent. These differences are most acute in countries where enrolments are low overall.

Educational 'ghettos' exist for girls and for boys, but boys have more and better choices than do girls. In vocational secondary schools in France in 1980, for every 100 boys, there were 5 girls in horticulture, 58 in arts and crafts and 14,000 in secretarial schools. Less than one girl per 100 boys registered for electrical or engineering trades training.

Data is based on 'enrolment *ratios*' – the proportion of eligible children attending schools – not rates (the actual number of children attending).

**Sources**: E. Bartunek, C. Bohm & I. Gross, 1984; V. Bodrova and R. Anker, 1985; CEC, **Supplement No.s 10** and **11**, 1982 and **14**, 1984; D. Davin, 1976; European Documentation, 1984; E.W. Fernea, 1985; M. McAndrew & J. Peers (n.d.); Pakistan, Ministry of Information and Broadcasting, **Women in Pakistan** (n.d.); E. Hong, 1983; IPPF, 'Youth' wallchart, 1985; UNESCO, **Women and Development**, 1981; UNICEF, **State of World's Children 1985**; US Department of Commerce, Census, **Illustrative Statistics**, 1980, and **Women of the World: Asia and Pacific**, 1985, **Latin America and Caribbean**, 1984, **Near East and North Africa**, 1985, **Sub-Saharan Africa**, 1984; World Bank, **World Tables**, 1984.

## 23 HIGHER EDUCATION

Women began entering university in the mid- to late-19th century in the USA, Canada, and the UK. Elsewhere in the world universities opened up in the post-World War Two period. Dramatic enrolment increases occurred, averaging 30 per cent of the total for poor countries worldwide. Between 1965 and 1985 estimated enrolment in Qatar and South Yemen increased from nought to 57 per cent and 19 per cent of the total respectively; in Guatemala from 9 per cent to 28 per cent; and in Brazil from 25 per cent to 48 per cent.

Today the world picture looks like this:

**Women's share of higher education,** 1985 UN estimates

| North America | 49 | Europe | 45 |
|---|---|---|---|
| Asia and USSR | 33 | Africa | 29 |
| Australia and New Zealand | 46 | Latin America and Caribbean | 45 |

The percentage of women faculty instructors has not increased nearly as dramatically as have student enrolments. In the USA in 1870 women represented 12 per cent of the teaching staff in universities; in 1880, 36 per cent; and in 1890, dropped to 20 per cent, averaging about one-quarter from then until today. The proportion has not increased since 1910.

In 1870 in the US, 21 per cent of all university students were women. Since then enrolment rates have fluctuated, peaking around 1930 and again in the 1940s. In 1944 50 per cent of BAs and MAs were awarded to women. A sharp postwar decline followed when war veterans flooded the schools. Women were encouraged to stay at home instead of competing with 'needier' men for school slots and jobs.

The terms university, college, post-secondary, third-level and higher education are used almost interchangeably in the literature; but the last two are the most inclusive.

**Sources**: G. Ashworth, 'Daughters' (n.d.); O. Carmichael, 1959; CEC, **Supplement Nos. 10 & 14**; Collier's Encyclopedia, 1985; Encyclopedia Britannica, 1985; E.W. Fernea, 1985; S. Harris, 1972; International Association of Universities, 1983; G. Kurian, 1984; J. L'Esperance, 1983; P.L. McGrath, 1976; P. Robertson, 1982; D. Robins-Mowry, 1983; A. Rossi and A. Calderwood, 1973; R.L. Sivard, 1985; UN Decade for Women, **(C) Education**, 1984; UNESCO, **Tendances**, 1984; UNICEF, **Situation in Kenya**, 1985; UN World Conference for Women, **Review and Evaluation: Education**, 1980, and **Statistical Abstract**, 1980; US Department of Commerce, Census, **Women in the World: Latin America and the Caribbean**, 1984; Urquhart and Buckley, 1965.

## 24 WORDS FOR WOMEN

The official UNESCO definition of literacy is 'the ability to read and write a sentence in daily life'. Using this definition, most industrialized countries report illiteracy rates of near nought per cent. This clearly ignores the problem of functional illiteracy, which is a serious and growing problem. Recent estimates in the USA, for example, conclude that 16 per cent of all whites, 44 per cent of all blacks, and 56 per cent of all Hispanics fall into the category of functional illiterates – and that 60 per cent of these are women.

There is a lot of international data on literacy rates, but illiteracy is also known to be widely under-reported – and underestimation usually means that information on women is more masked than that on men. It is generally safe to assume that illiteracy – and especially women's illiteracy – is a bigger problem than official statistics reveal.

The *gap* in illiteracy between men and women (not just absolute literacy rates) reveals the most about the relative burden of illiteracy borne by women. The map shows both indicators. In many countries few girls or boys go to school, and illiteracy for both runs high. But as adults, men have more opportunities than women to learn to read and write. Domestic duties and restrictive presumptions about women's roles often keep women too busy in, and confined to, the home for participation in adult literacy programmes. If literacy programmes are to help women, they must be designed for them.

There is little disagreement that literacy is a 'good thing', and that full literacy for all is an important social goal. However, some literacy programmes can be quite damaging – especially in countries with multiple languages and ethnic divisions. In many instances, ethnic children are taught in only one language, in an effort by the State to undermine ethnic identity. In other instances, certain groups have been excluded from the language of power; this is especially true of women. In Latin America, for example, more Indian men than women speak Spanish, and thus are better equipped to participate in national politics and power struggles.

**Sources**: K. Kelley, 1985; J.L. Scherer, 1983 and 1984; UN, **Compendium**, 1977; UN World Conference for Women, Statistical Abstract, 1985; UNESCO, **Statistical Yearbook**, 1983.

## 25 BREAD AND WATER

Fatigue is the most common chronic health problem for women. A male doctor in Mexico is quoted by Perdita Huston, 'Anaemia in women is extremely high. I don't really understand how they keep going'.

Anaemia is caused primarily by malnutrition. Half of all women, and two-thirds of all pregnant women in poor countries (not including China), suffer from iron-deficiency anaemia. It can be a mild condition, but does lead to higher maternal mortality and morbidity and a lowered work capacity. Anaemia affects women (and children) most because of their higher requirements for iron, in combination with their inadequate intake. Continuous childbearing and infection also contribute.

Women eat less and last, men and children are served first and best. It is estimated that there is a 42 per cent gap between the daily calorie requirement and actual daily calorie intake for women in India). Food taboos (for example no eggs during pregnancy for fear of developing a large foetus and having a painful birth) contribute to female malnutrition. Generally it is thought that women do not need – or deserve – as much food as others. The low birth weight of a mother's baby is an accurate reflection of her own poor physical condition.

Hard work, childbearing, and too little food cause anaemia; but 80 per cent of all disease in poor countries is caused by contaminated water. A billion people in the world lack safe drinking water; including 25 per cent of all city-dwellers and 71 per cent of urban-dwellers.

**Sources**: P. Blair, 1981; W.U. Chandler, 1984; PAHO, **Health Conditions**, 1982; E. Royston, 1982; UN Decade for Women, **Selected Statistics**, 1985; UNICEF, **State of World's Children**, 1984; WHO, **Prevalence of Anemia in Women**, 1979.

## 26 ILLNESS AND HEALTH

Women contribute most of the world's informal health care – far exceeding that given in the formal medical sector. Yet their own health needs have often been neglected or ignored by health planners.

Primary health care – local-level, semi-professional, preventative and low cost – is the key to improving the health of women around the world. Extending it to everyone in the world would cost $US 10 billion annually, one-twenty-fifth as much as the world spends on cigarettes. Nevertheless, this would represent a doubling of health expenditures for some countries.

As it is, public health spending priorities are skewed towards the inappropriate technology of the modern urban hospital, to which women seldom have access (figures from UNICEF).

| **Health expenditures and population served** Poor countries | | |
| --- | --- | --- |
| | (percentage of national health budgets) | (percentage of population) |
| PHC | 15 | 90 |
| Hospital care | 85 | 10 |

**Sources**: American Cancer Society, 1985; P. Blair, 1981; W.U. Chandler, 1984; **The Economist**, 23 February 1985; S. Okie, 1985; personal communication from National Cancer Institute, USA; C. Russell, 1985; **Science News**, 17 April 1982; UN Decade for Women, **Selected Statistics**, 1985, and **State of World's Women**, 1985; UNICEF, **State of World's Children**, 1984.

## 27 REFUGEES

Not only do women comprise the majority of refugees, but they also suffer greater hardships *as* refugees. Women as refugees are still expected to perform the tasks of childcare, cleaning, cooking and collecting fuel and water, but often without resources. Family survival depends on women's ability to adjust and compensate for impoverishment. Women also suffer considerable abuse. Rape by camp guards, border guards, and other refugees is all too common; the most publicized case of refugee rape is the constant marauding of refugee boats in the China Sea, where it is estimated that over 2400 women have been raped by pirates.

Though about 80 per cent of the world's refugees are women, and women also represent about 80 per cent of health care workers in refugee camps, they have little control over the administration of camps and little voice in the development of national and international refugee policies. Only about one-quarter of the UNHCR budget is earmarked for women's refugee programmes. More generally, women have little influence over the policies that bring about the wars and famines that produce refugees in the first place.

Countries that receive refugees are often in no position to help them. Somalia, for example, is facing drought at the same time that it is hosting over half a million Ethiopian refugees. The ratio of refugees to local population in Somalia is 1 in 7; in the Sudan, the ratio is 1 in 32. Generally, this means that life for refugees is almost as bad in the host country as in the country they fled. When resources are stretched thin, it is women, the most marginalized in the first place, who suffer first and most. Women have the smallest share of the 'resources pie' of the world; when the pie shrinks, women's losses are greatest.

Statistics on international refugees should be treated with caution. In the first place, refugee numbers are very fluid and reporting does not keep pace with fast-changing refugee situations. More important, it is known that refugee reporting is very susceptible to manipulation for political gain. Refugee statistics should be used for the general picture they offer, not the precision.

This map shows international refugees only. Many countries have large internal refugee populations that are as badly off as the international refugees. Cyprus, Angola, El Salvador, Nicaragua, and Guatemala, among others, have very large populations of internal refugees.

Sources: R. Aitchison, 1984; L. Bonnerjea, 1985; M. Kidron & R. Segal, 1984; Minority Rights Group, Refugee Dilemma, 1981; UN Decade for Women, (J) Refugee and Displaced Women; UNHCR, Fact Sheets, Refugees, 1984, 1985, and World Refugee Map, 1984; US Committee for Refugees, 1983.

## 28 POVERTY

Worldwide, the largest poverty groups are, first, women-headed households, and second, the elderly (a greater proportion of whom are women because women live longer than men). Together, these two groups represent on average 70 per cent of the poor in most countries in the world. Poverty is rapidly being feminized. The scattered statistics that are available tell the same story worldwide: in the USA, 78 per cent of all people living in poverty are women or children under the age of 18; in Australia, the proportion is 75 per cent; in Canada, 60 per cent of all women over age 65 live in poverty.

The reasons for women-headed households being poor can be found in the maps in the 'Work' section (Maps 15 through 20). Women who are solely responsible for their families often cannot go out to work because there are no childcare facilities available (or because childcare is too expensive). When women do work for wages, they get paid less, they are ghettoized into low-paying jobs with little job security, and have fewer job benefits. In agricultural economies, credit, money and land ownership are often denied women (see Map 21, 'Access to Means'); women are dependent on men for access to the resources and rewards of the formal economy. In the absence of men, women are cut off from access to resources.

There are great income differences between women-headed and men-headed households. In 1981 in the USA, the average income of women-headed households was $US 10,960; for men-headed households, it was $US 19,889; for husband-wife house-holds, it was $US 25,065. In Chile 29 per cent of women-headed households fall into the lowest income bracket, compared with 10 per cent of men-headed households.

Recessions and other economic hardships strike hardest at those with the least income: women and their children feel 'hard times' first and most. The poorer a family is, the larger is the proportion of income spent on necessities, such as food, fuel and health care. For poor families, then, any decline in income threatens survival.

The poorer women are, the more vulnerable they are to exploitation, especially prostitution. There is a very strong connection between women's poverty and prostitution.

The number of women-headed households is everywhere increasing rapidly. In rich countries divorce is the major cause of the rise in single-parent families (see Map 5, 'Single States'); in poor countries, it is due to both divorce and the migration (either seasonal or permanent) of men seeking work.

Sources: N. Banerjee, 1983; M. Buvinic, 1978; D. Dwyer, 1983; ILO, Women at Work, various issues; J. Massiah, 1983; R. Morgan, 1984; PRB, 'The changing American family', 1983; press reports; J. Schirmer, 1982; H. Scott, 1984; K. Stallard et al., 1983; UNICEF, Assignment Children, Spring 1980, and The State of the World's Children 1985, UN World Assembly on Aging, 1982; US Commission on Civil Rights, 1983; US Department of Commerce, Women of the World: A Chartbook, 1985; US Department of Labor, 'Time of change', 1984; WIN News, Summer 1985.

## 29 THE VOTE

Women are still not fully enfranchised worldwide. Despite growing protests, the Kuwaiti government refuses to grant women the vote; in a 1985 debate, the

Interpretation Committee of Kuwait's Ministry of Islamic Affairs concluded that, 'the nature of the electoral process befits men, who are endowed with ability and expertise: it is not permissible that women nominate women or men'. In Bhutan, a 'one vote per family' rule means that men almost exclusively claim that right. Hong Kong has property restrictions that prevent some men, and a lot of women, from voting. And in South Africa, black women and men are still denied the vote.

The biggest surge in voting rights came during the late 1950s – in the wake of decolonization. But in many countries women's suffrage is even more recent: in Lichtenstein, women only won the vote in 1984; in Jordan, it was in 1982.

Partly because women do not have such a long history of political participation they tend to vote less than men. In many countries, and in many families, there is little encouragement for women to act autonomously and politically.

When women do vote, they increasingly vote differently than men on certain issues. These differences in political attitudes first began to be noticed consistently in the mid-1970s in American elections. The 'gender gap' at the polls has since become an important factor in elections in the USA. Women's voting records show that they are more likely to favour stronger environmental protection regulation, gun control, abolition of the death penalty, and are more likely to vote against weapons build-ups.

Historical information on women's suffrage is often hard to interpret. In many cases there is simply no record in standard historical sources. More often the dates in various sources are conflicting. This is because in many countries *some* women had the vote before others – and different sources record different benchmarks. For this map, we mark suffrage from the date that *all* women won the vote on equal terms with each other and on equal terms with men.

**Sources**: S. Baxter & M. Lansing, 1983; D. Boulding, 1976; D. Butler et al., 1981; CEC, **European Women and Men**, 1983; Minority Rights Group, **Latin American Women**, 1983; National Commission on Working Women, 1984; UN Commission on the Status of Women (annual reports); US Department of State, **Reports** (various), 1984.

## 30 GOVERNMENT

The importance of women's recent gains in political power must be measured against the fact that even in the best cases women represent only about 25 per cent of elected national officials. In many countries women have *no* share of political power. This is certainly true in all countries ruled by militaries (since women are nowhere in power in militaries – see Map 32, 'Military Service'), and in many countries where women only recently won the vote. Lichtenstein, for example, has only one woman member of parliament, elected in 1986.

A widespread pattern shows women to have made some gains in lower levels of legislature, but to the excluded from the upper echelons where real power lies. The most obvious example of this is in the Eastern European countries:

**Number of women in Politburos**, 1985

| Bulgaria | 0 | Romania | 1 |
|---|---|---|---|
| China | 1 | USSR | 0 |
| Czechoslovakia | 0 | Vietnam | 0 |
| E. Germany | 0 | Yugoslavia | 1 |
| Poland | 1 | | |

When women do hold cabinet posts, they are often appointments in areas considered to lie within women's traditional interests – not considered to be very serious: women get appointed to be Ministers of Consumer Affairs, not Ministers of Defence. There are many countries where no woman has yet made it to the level of a cabinet position.

Women tend to fare better in local politics. They typically have better representation in municipal councils than in national bodies. In the national legislatures in Scandinavian countries, women had achieved over 20 per cent representation by the early 1970s. They remain in the lead today. The 1985 figures are: Denmark, 26 per cent; Finland, 31 per cent; Norway, 26 per cent; and Sweden, 29 per cent.

Data on women in government is generally reliable, and coverage is fairly good – but a surprising number of countries still do not collect or report data on this topic.

**Sources**: AFSC, 1984; G. Flanz, 1983; J. Lovenduski & J. Hills, 1981; J. & K. Macksey, 1975; M. Shaul, 1982; R.L. Sivard, 1985; UNECA, **Mozambique**, 1980; UN World Conference for Women, **Report**, 1980; **Women of Europe**, March 1984.

## 31 THE LAW

Cross-cultural data on crime must be treated with caution. For one thing, there is considerable variation in what type of behaviour is defined as 'criminal' – and definitions change over time. In addition, there is little uniformity in national governments' methods of reporting their 'crime rate' to international authorities: in some instances anyone who is arrested is listed as a 'criminal'; in other countries 'criminals' are those *convicted* of crimes. On this map the crime rate is based on arrest records.

In addition to these interpretation problems there are major gaps in international data on the law and its enforcement. Very little information is broken down according to gender. For example, while there is some data on reported crimes, there is no information on women as political prisoners. (Amnesty International, which is the primary group monitoring political prisoners, does not collect information by sex.) There is little information on women in police forces, though in the USA women reportedly comprise six per cent of police forces nationwide.

The little information that exists on women in prisons suggests that overall they comprise a very small proportion of inmates. In Pakistan women are less than one per cent of all prison inmates; in Sweden, two per cent; in the Netherlands and the UK, three per cent; in China, five per cent. Contrary to commonly held beliefs, women do not get off lightly in the courts: a 1975 study in the UK showed that five times as many women with no previous convictions were jailed as men with no previous convictions.

Women are a small but growing proportion of lawyers and judges. Here, too, job ghettoization exists. Women judges are much more likely than men to be appointed to family courts. Very few women rise to posts in the upper courts.

Sources: F. Adler, 1981; **Change International Reports**, various countries; Interpol, 1979-80; G. Kurian, 1984; R. Morgan, 1984; **New York Times**, 10 March 1985; Pakistan, Ministry of Information and Broadcasting, 1981; Statistics Sweden, 1985; US Department of Justice, 1983; **WIN News**, various issues; **Women of Europe**, various issues.

## 32 MILITARY SERVICE

All over the world, there is controversy about whether women should be allowed to participate in militaries – and if so, to what extent. In some countries women are completely excluded from military service; in others, women can join the military, but are restricted to the lowest levels in the power hierarchy and slotted into typically 'feminized' jobs.

Notions of femininity are at the centre of all arguments against allowing women into the military. Women are portrayed as a weaker species who must be protected – indeed, men are encouraged to fight for their country in order to 'protect' women. The idea of women serving in the military, then, is discordant with the ideals of behaviour for both men and women: women shouldn't be in the military because it is unfeminine, and because it undermines the rationales used to keep men as soldiers. The idea of women being allowed to serve in *combat* is considered to be even further beyond the pale. Ideologies about femininity and the inappropriateness of women in the military are virtually universal: the same arguments are used by revolutionary governments, Communist governments, free market governments, in rich countries and poor.

Among feminists, too, the issue of whether women should be in the military is controversial; much of the feminist debate focuses specifically on conscription. In some countries, women argue *against* the conscription of women on the grounds that they should not be compelled to join male institutions of violence; there has been strong anti-conscription rallying in Italy, Greece, East and West Germany, and the USA. Increasingly European governments facing a decline in military manpower are considering the conscription of women. Yet in other countries women have argued on the basis of equal rights that they *should* be conscripted. For example, the recent decision of the Nicaraguan government not to conscript women was taken by many women as a snub, given their service in combat in the struggle to overthrow Somoza.

When women do break into the ranks, they are usually confined to 'women's roles', which (as in society at large) tend to be the least skilled, the lowest paid and have the least potential for promotion. Most militaries use women to provide 'support services', as nurses, secretaries and communications aides.

It is generally true that military service brings some social and economic benefits; by excluding women from service, they are excluded from these benefits too. In many countries, the military is the goverment – which means that the government is exclusively male, and women are held at a great distance from power.

Sources: C. Enloe, 1983, and conversations with C. Enloe; N.L. Goldman, 1982; **Les Femmes et L'Armée**, 1981; Minerva (quarterly); Minority Rights Group, **Latin American Women**, 1983; R. Morgan, 1984; NATO, 1984; S. Urdag, 1984; **Women of Europe**, various issues.

## 33 BODY AND MIND

The status of women in the health and education professions reflects an observation made by Margaret Mead about men's work and women's work: 'There are villages in which men fish and women weave, and those in which women fish and men weave, but in either type of village, the work done by men is valued higher than the work done by women.' In both health and education, the ranks with the greatest numbers of women – nursing and pre-primary school education – have the lowest status.

In most countries more than 90 per cent of nurses are women. In a few places, such as the UK and the USA, the proportion of male nurses is slowly increasing. And when this happens, the men rise to the top: although they are a minority of all nurses, they hold a disproportionate share of senior nursing posts – and nursing unions and organizations are generally dominated by the few men in them. In a few countries severe restrictions imposed on women's education and their activities outside the home has meant that nursing has never been feminized.

The proportion of women doctors worldwide has been rising steadily since World War Two, with the greatest increases appearing in the Communist countries – this is the result of a deliberate policy, and now in some parts of Eastern Europe the majority of doctors are women.

Many countries, notably in Europe and the USA, fail to report educational staff data to UNESCO, the only agency that keeps track of this information internationally. Thus on the education 'ladders' graphic there are some surprising countries for which the data is listed as 'unknown' – entirely the result of national policy on reporting to the UN.

Information on the proportion of women in the various parts of the health professions is surprisingly hard to find. The World Health Organization does not collect or report this data (with the exception of one listing made in 1977). Although it would seem an easy task to collect information on women as nurses and doctors (since health professionals everywhere are registered with the national health authorities), we were told by WHO that this information was 'not considered important to collect'.

Information on the important role of women as primary health-care providers is included on several maps, especially Map 11, 'Birth Care'.

Sources: Bui Dang Ha Doan, 1979; International Council of Nurses, 1983; G. Lapidus, 1978; R. Morgan, 1984; J. Salvage, 1985; Statistical Abstract of Latin America, 1982; State Statistical Bureau, China, 1984; UN, Compendium, 1980; UN Decade for Women, Selected Statistics, 1985; UNESCO, Statistical Yearbook, 1981, 1983; US Department of Commerce, Statistical Abstract, 1984; WHO, World Health Statistics, 1983;

## 34 THE MEDIA

In the USA there is only one mass-media magazine owned and operated by women (Ms.). So-called 'women's' magazines are owned by men, almost always published by men, and usually edited by men. By contrast, all the feminist print media listed in 'The Furthest Reach' graphic are owned and operated by women. Not surprisingly the sex magazines are owned and operated almost completely by men.

At their best, 'women's magazines' provide a wealth of practical information; at their worst they aggressively reinforce what is most negative about traditional notions of femininity. It matters; 29,500,000 people received the magazines listed in the 'Reach' graphic alone. Compare this with the 943,000 recipients of the feminist magazines and the 13.8 million pornography readers listed.

Much of the pornography industry is outside the regular economy and thus is hard to document. Figures used to estimate its size are thought to be very low (the US industry is estimated as $US 8 billion in 1984). The industry barely existed before the 1960s, but its growth since then has been explosive. There are well over 165 pornographic magazines in the USA alone and their content is increasingly violent and explicit, and the women featured continue to be exploited. One issue of *Penthouse* magazine featuring old photographs of the then-Miss America sold 10 million copies, netted the publisher $US 37 million and Miss America nothing but the loss of her crown for unbecoming behaviour. A content analysis of pornographic paperbacks found that depictions of rape had doubled between 1968 and 1974; depictions of bondage and domination have also increased dramatically. Pornography is anathema because it dehumanizes people; it has nothing to do with healthy adult sexuality.

For many women, especially the millions of poor and illiterate women, print media is irrelevant to their lives. Radio is the most accessible of all the media; in Europe and parts of Africa, for example, more women listen to radio than do men.

Sources: M.L. Allen, 1985; E.L. Anani, 1981; Austrian Federal Ministry (n.d.); B.H. Bagdikian, 1983; S. Brownmiller, 1975; CEC, Women of Europe, various issues; Clearinghouse on Development Communication, 1983; Consumers Association of Penang, 1982; G.F. Epstein & R. L. Coser, 1984; M. Gallagher, 1981; J. Gay, 1983; IMS/Ayer, 1985; ISIS, 'Women and the media', 1981, and 'Women and visual images', 1983; J. Koten & R. Johnson, 1985; L. Lederer, 1980; Media Development, 1984; R. Morgan, 1984; K. Newland, 1979; Pakistan, Ministry of Information and Broadcasting, 1982; NOW, 1984; S. Pervaiz (n.d.); D.E. Russell, 1982; Ulrich's International, 1985; US News and World Report (weekly).

## 35 BEAUTY BEAT

In addition to the two major international contests, hundreds of beauty contests are held around the world each year. Contests present women and 'beauty' as commodities – and are in this way directly related to the images of women presented in pornography and in the mass media. A wide range of countries participate in the beauty beat. Ideologies of beauty – and of women as objects of beauty – transcend all sorts of other political and economic differences. The beauty beat seems to be gathering momentum. Beauty contests were begun in China in 1985; Hungary also started to hold contests in 1985; in 1983 Poland was the first Eastern bloc country to send a contestant to Miss World. Muslim countries are the only ones that do not host beauty contests.

Although beauty contests are supposed to be non-political 'entertainment', they are at the centre of much controversy and acrimony. Feminists uniformly condemn beauty contests. Criticism is also more widespread – for example in 1984 the BBC ended coverage of beauty contests, calling them 'anachronistic and offensive'. Hosting a pageant can be very controversial – especially in poorer countries, since governments spend a lot of money preparing sites and promoting contests held in their country; the sites of beauty contests are almost always the sites of protests. Most contests are riven with internal contradictions: there is always a furore, for example, when it is discovered that one of the contestants has posed nude for modelling or pornography magazines, or that one of the contestants had a teenage pregnancy. Every year there are a number of beauty queens deposed for one transgression or another.

A staggering amount of money and suffering is spent on the pursuit of beauty. Some cosmetic surgery is essential – reconstruction following surgery, for example. But the overwhelming proportion of cosmetic surgery is non-essential, and indicates the extent to which women have been socialized to pursue the elusive ideal of beauty at any cost.

**Sources**: Christian Science Monitor, 20 March 1984; Drug and Cosmetic Industry, various issues; Forbes, 18 June 1984; Miss Universe, 1985; Miss World, 1985; Newsweek, 'Health supplement', Fall 1985; R. Stern, 1982.

## 36 SEX FOR SALE

Prostitution is as old as patriarchy. Prostitution flourishes in an economic context where women are paid less than men for their labour power, and the one commodity they possess for which men are willing to pay a price is their bodies. Prostitution exists everywhere. But to say simply that it 'exists' masks the processes through which prostitution is perpetuated – economic processes, male networks of control and trade in women, and the violence and coercion that permeates all systems of prostitution.

International traffic in women is flourishing; trafficking means simply the transport, exchange, and sale of women through networks set up and controlled by men. Most trafficking takes one of three forms. Firstly, women who are already prostitutes in one country are often 'exchanged' to another country. Since most prostitutes are in the control of pimps, they have no say in these transfers – they are merely commodities being exchanged between men. Secondly, girls are often sold into prostitution by poor families; the families are in some instances aware that they are selling their daughter into prostitution, but more often than not they are told that the child will be employed as a domestic servant in a patron's home. Once prostituted, the already low value of girls to their families drops even lower. Thirdly, there is evidence of women being recruited from poverty under false pretences – they are hired to be 'waitresses' or 'domestic servants', and are then forced into prostitution. Much of the international traffic in women takes the form of sexual slavery.

Marriage bureaux which offer women for sale to prospective husbands – a supposedly legitimate business – are often little more than fronts for prostitute networks. Women bought through these marriage brokers are often put to work as prostitutes in foreign countries. Even when marriage bureaux do not serve to supply prostitute networks, the fact that they are established in order to sell women closely relates them to the business of prostitution.

Sex tourism is literally that: hundred of thousands of men each year flock to various centres in Southeast Asia for 'sex holidays'. Tours are arranged by 'legitimate' travel operators in Japan, West Germany and Scandinavia, who for one all-in price offer airfare, a hotel room and a pre-arranged number of women 'for the men to do as they like with'. The women who are offered up for these sex tours are often kept in conditions of near-slavery, and one common practice is to parade women with numbers around their necks through hotel viewing rooms so the men can pick whom they want. Many of the prostitutes are children: there are an estimated 30,000 prostitutes in Bangkok under the age of 16, for example. Sex tourism is big business, and in most instances has the implicit (or even direct) support of the host government: sex tourism is a major source of foreign currency and, in many cases, props up a failing economy. Sex tourism in many countries started with brothels established to service military bases.

Prostitution and/or related activities are illegal in most countries. Even where prostitution itself is technically not a crime, it is always the prostitutes – not the pimps or customers – who are harassed or arrested. Nowhere is there legal protection for prostitutes, nor prosecution of the men who exploit prostitutes.

**Sources**: Asian Women's Association, 1980; K. Barry, 1984; conversations with K. Barry; K. Barry, C. Bunch & S. Castley, 1984; Canadian Advisory Council, 1984; Connexions, various issues; ISIS 'Prostitution: who pays?', 1984; R. Morgan, 1984; New York Times, 24 June 1985; V. Ohse, 1984; P. Phongpaichit, 1982; Spare Rib, Oct 1985; K. Thitsa, 1980; UN Economic and Social Council, 1982 and 1983; Washington Post, 3 March 1985; Women in Europe, various issues.

## 37 RAPE

Rape is not uncontrolled lust and it is not 'having sex'. Rape is a violent act done by a man to a woman – sometimes to a child – in order to establish power over her or women in general. It is committed mostly when and where men can get away with it – often in the home – and without regard to a woman's age or appearance. It is not true that most rapes are committed by strangers, only on pretty women, when the woman is 'asking for it'. If a woman fights back she may be seriously injured or killed; but if she doesn't, she is assumed to have been complicit in the act. This puts women in a no-win situation. Because some men rape, all women are threatened by rape and are thus unable to move about freely.

Rape is not an impulse act in most cases. In the USA one study showed 90 per cent of gang rapes, 83 per cent of pair rapes and 58 per cent of single rapes to be premeditated. Most cultures either condone rape or legitimize it by ignoring it in reality and enjoying it in fantasy. As some feminists say, 'Pornography is the theory, rape is the practice'. The 'ideal' woman in the media's image is very similar to the 'ideal' rape victim: docile, selfless, a sex object.

The Dublin rape crisis centre in Ireland experienced a two-fold increase in women seeking help between 1983 and 1984. As rape rates and reporting increase, pressure by women's groups is forcing legal systems to respond to rape as a serious social problem. In many countries, however, the legal system *is* part of the problem. Institutional rape by jail guards and police in prisons, by 'orderlies' in mental hospitals, by authorities in refugee camps (see Notes to Map 27, 'Refugees'), is used to remind women of their powerlessness and to keep them powerless. It is also used by men against other men, as in war: the conquering soldier rapes and plunders to establish his dominance over his counterpart through property. Where rape *is* severely punished, as in Muslim countries, the crime is seen as an affront to the possessing male, not to the woman victim. In every case the punishment of rape is contingent on its being reported, which in turn is contingent upon a woman being able to recognize rape as the unjustifiable assault it is, not something deserved – particularly as in wife-rape or 'date-rape'. Men and women still assume on some level that the rape victim is guilty of enticement or some other attitude which legitimately provokes a man to rape. Women hesitate to report rape for other reasons, too: fear of reprisal from her attacker or his compatriots and lack of faith in the criminal justice system which might put *her* on trial for *her sexuality*. In the USA ten rapes are reported every hour. This probably represents – at a conservative estimate – ten per cent of those occurring.

Historically the criminalization of rape was not designed to protect women but to protect male property. The rape of a man's wife or daughter was and is considered a serious crime; wife-as-property lingers as a category in the law. This is evident in the recent and still rare acceptance of wife-rape as prosecutable. (You cannot violate the rights of someone who – in your mind or in the law – has no independent civil rights of her own.) Some countries only recognize wife-rape when a husband and wife are *separated*, thereby failing to accept the basic concept. Canada and Yugoslavia are examples. In general socialist law protects wives from rape most, Muslim law the least. The insistence by some on calling wife-rape 'spousal rape' begs the issue, which is most certainly *not* gender-neutral.

Because rape is so under-reported, statistics are unreliable. This is as true of small-sample studies as it is of Interpol statistics. There is extreme hesitancy on the part of women to report rape, and a certain lack of determination by authorities to collect accurate numbers. The definition of 'sex offences' varies widely too. The 'sex offence' figure for the USA includes only rape, while in other countries, prostitution, the traffic in women and other crimes are included. It is thus difficult to make any generalizations about cultural patterns based on these statistics.

**Sources**: S. Brownmiller, 1975; A.W. Burgess, 1985; Canadian Advisory Council, 'Sexual assault', 1985; M. Capuzzo, 1984; Interpol, 1979-80; ISIS, 'Organizing against Rape', 1979; G. Kurian, 1984; M.A. Largen, 1985; London Rape Crisis Centre; J. Mann, 1985; **Newsweek**, 1985, **New York Times**, 29 December 1984; **Off Our Backs**, Aug/Sept, 1984; D.E. Russell, 1982; D.E. Russell & N. Van der Ven, 1984; US Department of Justice, 1983; WAP, 1985; **Washington Post**, 20 August 1985; H. Wheeler, 1985; **WIN News** (quarterly); Women's History Resource Centre; K. Yllo and D. Finkelhor, 1985.

## 38 CHANNELS OF CHANGE

Women have created powerful channels of change over the past decade. The women's non-governmental organizations (NGOs) took key roles in forging resolutions and recommendations at the three UN Decade of Women conferences. In most countries women's political action groups have become important lobbying forces. Women's research centres have been founded in more than 25 countries.

They have fared less well inside conventional channels. Only a few governments have established women's ministries – and in some (for example Canada), the minister is a man. Women are not represented in senior posts or policy-making positions within any of the major international agencies.

In most countries women have been forming professional and political organiza-tions since the mid-19th century. Suffrage organizations began in the 1860s in England and the USA, and in the 1880s and 1990s in the Scandinavian countries. Some of the earliest international women's organizations were created around peace issues. A note of irony is that in some women's organizations, men hold the top posts: the

League of Women Voters (US) for example, founded in 1920, just elected – in 1986 – a man as its executive director.

**Sources**: E. Boulding, 1977, and 1980; G.F. Epstein & R. L. Coser, 1984; R.J. Evans, 1977; ILO, **Women at Work**, Vol. 1, 1984; International Women's Tribune Centre, 'Women's centers', 1982; ISIS, **Women in Development**, 1983; **New York Times**, 11 September 1985; UN, **Report of the World Conference**, 1975; UN Decade for Women, **Report of the Secretary-General**, 1985, and **Report of the World Conference**, 1985, UN World Conference for Women, **Descriptive List**, 1980, and **Report**, 1980; US Congress, **Women in Development**, 1984.

## 39 PROTESTS

Women's protests are not new – women have always struggled against their oppression. Contemporary movements have links back to early women textile-workers' strikes, and prohibition and temperance movements.

Many women's street demonstrations have been called to protest for reproductive rights and legal equality, and against male violence. Recently, in the Arab states women have organized against repressive 'Family Codes'. In Iceland women organized a one-day strike (in 1975 and again in 1985) against 'male privilege'.

The list of street demonstrations was gleaned from the back-issues of several feminist magazines and newspaper indexes – but we know it is not complete. We have not mapped the various and numerous 'Take Back the Night' marches that have occurred throughout Europe, Australia, Canada, and the USA.

**Sources**: Connexions (quarterly); R. Kamel, 1985; R. Morgan, 1984; **New Internationalist**, various issues; New Internationalist, **Women: A World Report**, 1985; Puget Sound Women's Peace Camp, 1985; **Spare Rib**, various issues; **Women's Peace Alliance**, June 1985.

## 40 MAPPING THE PATRIARCHY

The collection and dissemination of statistics about people is political. The collecting agency must decide how, where and why to collect information, and what it should be. These choices are made, by and large, by men. As a result women are often absent from compendia of international statistics. Where information on women is included it is often incomplete and concerns either what the collectors consider important about women or what is most easily obtained. (It is also true that certain information about men – for example men as fathers – is not collected.)

The lack of data on issues of concern to women certainly frustrates researchers, but its implications go far beyond that. Decisions affecting millions of people – as in international development planning – hinge on the nature of the information used by the decision-makers. The failure to recognize that women are half the labour force, all of the reproducing force and almost all of the food preparation force – among other things – has contributed to failure of many development schemes by effectively keeping out of the picture half of the society supposedly being helped.

**Sources**: E. Boulding, 1976; IPPF wallchart, 1985; B. Rogers, 1980; UN Decade for Women, (**B**) **Health and Nutrition**, 1984, and **Selected Statistics** 1985; USAID, 1984.

# BIBLIOGRAPHY

## A

ABEILLE, Barbara, **A Study of Female Life in Mauritania**, Washington DC, Office of Women in Development, USAID (US Agency for International Development), 1979.

ACHARYA, Meena, *et al.*, **The Status of Women in Nepal**, USAID, 1979.

ADLER, Freda, ed., **The Incidence of Female Criminality in the Contemporary World**, New York, New York University Press, 1981.

AFSC (American Friends Services Committee), **Women's Newsletter** (quarterly), Philadelphia.

AITCHISON, Roberta, 'Reluctant witnesses: the sexual abuse of refugee women in Djibouti', **Cultural Survival Quarterly**, Vol. 8, No. 2, 1984.

ALLEN, Martha Leslie, ed., **Index/Directory of Women's Media**, Washington DC, Women's Institute for Freedom of the Press, 1985.

ANANI, Elma Lititia, *et al.*, **Women and the Mass Media in Africa: Case Studies from Sierra Leone, the Niger, and Egypt**, Addis Ababa, UNECA (UN Economic Council for Africa), 1981

ANDREWS, Alice, 'Revised analysis of a status-of-women index'. Paper presented to the Association of American Geographers, April 1982.

ANDREWS, Alice, 'Toward a status-of-women index', **Professional Geographer**, Vol. 34, No. 1, February 1982.

ASHWORTH, Georgina, 'Asking women but not feminists', **Spare Rib**, No. 147, London, October 1984.
– ed., 'Daughters of the nightmare: Caribbean women', **Change International Reports**, London, n.d.

Asian Women's Association, 'Prostitution tourism', **Asian Women's Liberation**, Vol. 3, 1980.

Austrian Federal Ministry for Social Affairs, **Women and Media in Austria: International and National Activities**, Vienna, Austrian Federal Ministry for Social Affairs, n.d.

## B

BAGDIKIAN, Ben H., **The Media Monopoly**, Boston, Beacon Press, 1983.

BANERJEE, Nirmala, 'Women and poverty: report on a workshop', **Economic and Political Weekly**, 1 October 1983.

BARRY, Kathleen, **Female Sexual Slavery**, New York, New York University Press, 1984 (revised edition).

BARRY, Kathleen, Charlotte Bunch and Shirley Castley, eds., **International Feminism: Networking Against Female Sexual Slavery**, New York, 1984.

BARTUNEK, E., C. Bohm and Inge Gross, **The Economic Role of Women in Austria**, Vienna, Austrian Federal Ministry of Social Affairs, 1984.

BAXTER, Sandra and Marjorie Lansing, **Women and Politics: The Visible Majority**, Ann Arbor, University of Michigan, 1983.

BECK, Lois and Nikki Keddie, **Women in the Muslim World**, Cambridge MA., Harvard University Press, 1978.

BENERIA, Lourdes, 'Women and rural development – Morocco', **Cultural Survival Quarterly**, Vol. 8, No. 2, 1984.

BODROVA, V. and R. Anker, eds., **Working Women in Socialist Countries: The Fertility Question**, Geneva, ILO (International Labour Office), 1985.

BONNERJEA, Lucy, **Shaming the World: The Needs of Refugee Women**, London, Change Reports, 1985.

BOSERUP, Ester and Christina Liljencrantz, **Integration of Women in Development**, New York, UNDP (UN Development Programme), 1975.

Boston Women's Health Book Collective (file materials).

BOULDING, Elise, **Handbook on International Data on Women**, New York, Sage Publications, 1976.
– **Women in the Twentieth Century World**, New York, Sage Publications, 1977.
– **Women: The Fifth World**, Foreign Policy Association Headline Series, No. 248, 1980.

BROWN, Judith E., 'Polygyny and family planning in sub-Saharan Africa', **Studies in Family Planning**, Vol. 12, No.s 8/9, Aug/Sept 1981.

BROWNMILLER, Susan, **Against Our Will: Men, Women and Rape**, New York, Simon & Schuster, 1975.

BUI DANG HA DOAN, 'Women in the health professions', **World Health Statistics Quarterly**, Vol. 32, No. 2, 1979.

BURGESS, Anne Wolbert, **Rape and Sexual Assault – A Research Handbook**, New York, Garland Publishing, 1985.

BUTLER, D., *et al.*, **Democracy at the Polls**, Washington DC, American Enterprise Institute, 1981.

BUVINIC, Mayra, *et al.*, **Women and Poverty in the Third World**, Baltimore, Johns Hopkins University Press, 1983.

BUVINIC, Mayra, *et al.*, **Women-Headed Households: The Ignored Factor in Development Planning**, USAID, 1978.

## C

CAIN, Mead, 'Son preference and economic security', **World Bank Staff Working Papers**, No. 682, 1984.

Canadian Advisory Council on the Status of Women, **Prostitution in Canada**, March 1984.
– **Sexual Assault**, Ottawa, 1985.
– **Wife Battering**, Toronto, 1985.

CAPLAN, Patricia and Janet Bujra, eds., **Women United, Women Divided – Comparative Studies of Ten Contemporary Cultures**, Bloomington, Indiana University Press, 1982.

CAPUZZO, Mike, 'Rape within marriage', **Boston Globe**, 29 December 1984.

CARMICHAEL, Oliver, **Universities: Commonwealth and American**, New York, Harper & Row, 1959.

CEC (Commission of the European Communities), **Equal Opportunity for Working Women**, Brussels, CEC, 1980.
– **European Women and Men**, Brussels, CEC, 1984.
– **European Women and Men in 1983**, Brussels, CEC, 1983.
– **Supplement No. 10 to Women of Europe**, 'Women in statistics', Brussels, CEC, 1982.
– **Supplement No. 11 to Women of Europe**, 'Women in Portugal', Brussels, CEC, 1982.
– **Supplement No. 13 to Women of Europe**, 'Women in agriculture', Brussels, CEC, 1983.
– **Supplement No. 15 to Women of Europe**, 'Women at work in the

European Community', Brussels, CEC, 1984.
– **Supplement No. 17 to Women of Europe**, 'Women and development', Brussels, CEC, 1984.

CHANDLER, W. U., 'Improving world health: a least cost strategy', **Worldwatch Paper**, No. 59, Washington DC, Worldwatch Institute, 1984.

CHAPKIS, W., ed., **Loaded Questions: Women in the Military**, Amsterdam, Transnational Institute; Washington DC, Institute for Policy Studies, 1981.

CHAPKIS, Wendy and Cynthia Enloe, eds., **Of Common Cloth: Women in the Global Textile Industry**, Amsterdam, Transnational Institute; Washington DC, Institute for Policy Studies, 1983.

CHOJNACKA, Helen, 'Polygyny and the rate of population growth', **Population Studies**, Vol. 34, No. 1, Mar 1980.

**Christian Science Monitor**, 'Drugs in cosmetics', 20 March 1984.

CLOUD, Kathleen, **Sex Roles in Food Production and Food Distribution Systems in the Sahel**, Tucson, University of Arizona and USAID, 1977.

**Collier's Encyclopedia**, New York, Macmillan Educational Company, 1983.

**Connexions: An International Women's Quarterly**, People's Translation Service, Oakland, California.

Consumers Association of Penang, **Abuse of Women in the Media**, Penang, Consumers Association, 1982.

COOK, Rebecca, Napier Pillai and Bernard Dickens, **Abortion Laws in the Commonwealth Carribean. Report of Team Visit: Barbados, Trinidad and Tobago**, London, IPPF (International Planned Parenthood Federation), 1977.

Council of Europe, **Family Formation and Dissolution**, European Population Conference, 1982.
– **Midwives in Europe**, 1975.

CREW (Centre for Research on European Women), **Reports: Newsbulletin** (monthly), Brussels.

CROPPER, Angela, **The Integration of Women in Development for the Windward and Leeward Islands of the Caribbean**, University of the West Indies, March 1980.

# D

DAVIN, Delia, **Woman-Work**, Oxford, Clarendon Press, 1976.

DEERE, Carmen Diana and Magdalena Leon de Leal, 'Women in Andean agriculture', **Women, Work and Development**, No. 4, Geneva, ILO, 1982.

**Demography** (monthly), Washington DC.

DIXON, Ruth, **Rural Women at Work**, Baltimore, Johns Hopkins University Press, 1978.

**Drug Store News**, 'Birth control pills', 15 November 1982.

**Drugs and Cosmetic Industry** (monthly), New York.

DWYER, Daisy, **Women and Income in the Third World**, Population Council Working Paper No. 18, New York, 1983.

# E

**The Economist** (weekly), London.

EL SAADAWI, Nawal, **The Hidden Face of Eve: Women in the Arab World**, trans. Sherif Hetata, London, Zed Press, 1980.

**Encyclopaedia Britannica**, 1985.

ENLOE, Cynthia, **Does Khaki Become You? The Militarization of Women's Lives**, London, Pluto Press; Boston, South End Press, 1983.

EPSTEIN, Cynthia Fuchs and Rose Lamb Coser, **Access to Power: Cross-National Studies of Women and Elites**, London, George Allen & Unwin, 1984.

European Documentation, **Women in the European Community**, Luxembourg, 1984.

Eurostat, **Economic and Social Position of Women in the Community**, London, 1980.

EVANS, Richard J., **The Feminists**, New York, Croom Helm, 1977

# F

**Family Planning in the 1980s**, Report of the International Conference on Family Planning in the 1980s, Jakarta, 1981.

FAO (Food and Agriculture Organization of the United Nations), **Information Note on Women in Agriculture**, Rome, FAO, 1983.
– **The Legal Status of Rural Women**, Economic and Social Development Paper No. 9, 1979.

FERNEA, Elizabeth W., **Women and the Family in the Middle East**, Austin, University of Texas Press, 1985.

FESHBACH, Murray, 'The Soviet Union: population trends and dilemmas', **Population Bulletin**, Vol. 37, No. 3, Washington DC, Population Reference Bureau, 1982.

FLANZ, Gisbert, **Comparative Women's Rights and Political Participation in Europe**, New York, Transnational Publications, 1983.

**Forbes**, 'Marketing Miss Universe vs. Miss America', 18 June 1984.

FUENTES, Annette and Barbara Ehrenreich, **Women in the Global Factory**, Boston, South End Press, 1983.

# G

GALLAGHER, Margaret, **Unequal Opportunities – The Case of Women and the Media**, Paris, UNESCO, 1981.

GAY, Jill, 'Sweet darlings in the Media', **Multinational Monitor**, Vol. 4, No. 8, Aug 1983.

George Washington University Medical Centre, 'Law and policy', **Population Reports**, Series E, No. 3, Washington DC, 1976.
– 'Pregnancy termination', **Population Reports**, Series F, No. 1, Washington DC, 1973.

GILL, Margaret and Joycelin Massiah, **Women, Work and Development**, Women in the Caribbean Project, Vol. 6, 1984.

GOLDMAN, Nancy Loring, ed., **Female Soldiers – Combatants or Non-Combatants?**, London, Greenwood Press, 1982.

GOLDSCHMIDT-CLERMONT, L., **Unpaid Work in the Household**, Geneva, ILO, 1983.

DE GRAFT-JOHNSON, K.T., **Family Formation in Developing Countries**, World Fertility Survey Conference, 1980.

# H

HAMILTON, Sahni, Barry Popkin and Deborah Spicer, **Women and Nutrition in Third World Countries**, New York, Praeger Publishers, 1984.

HARRIS, Seymour, **A Statistical Portrait of Higher Education**, New York, McGraw Hill, 1972.

HAUPT, Arthur and Thomas T. Kane, **Population Handbook, International Edition**, Washington DC, Population Reference Bureau, 1982.

HECKATHORN, Cindy, 'Agrarian reform: a women's issue at mid-decade', **Hunger Notes**, Vol. 5, No. 10, Mar 1980.

HELMORE, Kristin, 'The neglected resource: women in the developing world', **Christian Science Monitor**, 17–20 December 1985.

HIRSCHON, Renee, ed., **Women and Property – Women as Property**, London, Croom Helm, 1984.

HONG, Evelyn, ed., **Malaysian Women: Problems and Issues**, Penang, Consumers Association of Penang, 1983.

HOSKEN, Fran, **Female Sexual Mutilations: The Facts and Proposals for Action – An Action Guide**, Lexington, MA, Women's International News, 1980.
– **The Hosken Report: Genital and Sexual Mutilation of Females**, Lexington MA, Women's International News, 1982 (third revised edition).
– 'Women and health: genital and sexual mutilation of females', **International Journal of Women's Studies**, Vol. 3, No. 3, May/June 1980.

**Hunger Notes**, Newsletter of the World Hunger Education Service (monthly), Washington DC.

HUSTON, Perdita, **Message From the Village**, New York, Unipub,

978.
Third World Women Speak Out: Interviews in Six Countries on Change, Development, and Basic Needs, New York, Praeger Publishers, 1979.

LO (International Labour Office), **Chart of Ratifications of International Labour Conventions**, Geneva, 1984.
**Problems of Women Non-Manual Workers**, Geneva, 1981.
**Womanpower**, Geneva, 1975.
**Women at Work** (twice yearly), Geneva.
**Women in Rural Development: Critical Issues**, Geneva, 1981.
**Work and Family Life**, Geneva.
**World Labour Report**, Geneva, 1985.
**Yearbook of Labour Statistics** (annual), Geneva.

International Council of Nurses, **Information and Data on Nursing in Countries of ICN Member Associations**, 1983.

International Reference Centre for Abortion Research, Transnational Family Research Institute, **Abortion Research Notes**, Vol. 12, No.s 1 & , July 1983; Vol. 13, No.s 1 & 2, July 1984.

International Women's Tribune Centre, 'Women and water', Newsletter No. 20, third quarter, New York, 1982.
'Women's centres world-wide', The Tribune, No. 19, 1982.

Interpol, **International Crime Statistics, 1979–1980**.

PPF (International Planned Parenthood Federation), 'Women: Progress towards equality' (wallchart), London, IPPF, 1985.
'Youth in society' (wallchart), London, IPPF, 1985.

**PPF News** (monthly), London.

SIS, 'Migrant women', **International Bulletin**, No. 14, 1980.
'Motherhood', **International Bulletin**, No. 23, June 1982.
'Organizing against rape', **International Bulletin**, No. 12, 1979.
'Prostitution: who pays?', **Women's World**, No. 3, Sept 1984.
'Third international meeting – women and health', International Bulletin, No. 20, 1981.
'Women and the media', **International Bulletin**, No. 18, 1981.
'Women and visual images', **International Bulletin**, No. 27, 1983.
**Women in Development: A resource Guide for Organization and Action**, Geneva, 1983.
''Women, land and food production', International Bulletin, No. 11, 979.

SLAM, Mahmuda, 'Social norms, institutions, and status of women', n Women for Women Research and Study Group, ed., **Situation of Women in Bangladesh**, Dacca, Women for Women/UNICEF, 1977.

**K**

AMEL, Rachel, 'Is a women's peace movement taking root?', **AFSC (American Friends Service Committee) Women's Newsletter**, Winter, 985.

ELLEY, Kevin, 'All over the US, the lights of literacy are going out', Guardian, 27 March 1985.

IDRON, Michael and Ronald Segal, **The New State of the World Atlas**, London, Pan; New York, Simon & Schuster, 1984.

URIAN, George, ed., **The New Book of World Rankings**, New York, Facts on File Publications, 1984.

UTZNER, Patricia L., 'Women and the problem of hunger', **Hunger Notes**, Vol. 7, No. 8, January 1982.

ANGEN, Mary Anne, 'The anti-rape movement: past and present', in urgess, A.W., **Rape and Sexual Assault**, op. cit.

APIDUS, Gail, **Women in Soviet Society**, Berkeley, University of California Press, 1978.

EGHORN, Lisa and Mary Roodkowssky, **Who Really Starves? Women and World Hunger**, New York, Friendship Press, 1977.

EMKE, Christiane, 'Women and politics in East Germany', **Socialist Review**, No. 81, May–June 1985.

ERMAN, Lisa, et al., 'State legislation on domestic violence', Response, Vol. 6, 1983.

**Les Femmes et L'Armée**, Lyons, 1981.

L'ESPERANCE, Jeanne, **The Widening Sphere: Women in Canada, 1870–1940**, Ottawa, Public Archives of Canada, 1983.

LOVENDUSKI, J. and J. Hills, **The Politics of the Second Electorate**, Boston, Routledge & Kegan Paul, 1981.

**M**

MACKSEY, Joan and Kenneth Macksey, **The Book of Women's Achievements**, New York, Stein & Day, 1975.

MAMLOUK, Maria, **Knowledge and Use of Contraception in Twenty Developing Countries**, Population Reference Bureau, Reports on the World Fertility Survey, No. 3, 1982.

**Manushi** (monthly), Delhi.

MASSIAH, Joycelin, **Women as Heads of Household in the Carribbean**, UNESCO, 1983.

MAYER, Ann Elizabeth, 'Law and women in the Middle East', **Cultural Survival Quarterly**, Vol. 8, No. 2, Summer 1984.

MCANDREW, Maggie and Jo Peers, 'The new Soviet woman: model or myth?', **Change International Reports**, London, n.d.

MCAULEY, Alastair, **Women's Work and Wages in the Soviet Union**, London, George Allen & Unwin, 1981.

MCGRATH, Patricia L, 'The unfinished assignment: equal education for women', **Worldwatch Papers**, No. 7, Washington DC, Worldwatch Institute, 1976.

**Media Development**, 'Women and media', Vol. XXXI, No. 2, 1984.

MEYER, Jurgen, **Report on the International Status of Marital Rape**, courtesy of Women's History Research Centre, National Clearinghouse on Marital Rape, Berkeley, California.

**Migration Today** (quarterly), New York.

**Minerva: Quarterly Report on Women and the Military**, Washington DC.

Minority Rights Group, **Arab Women**, Report No. 27, London, 1983 (revised).
– **Female Circumcision, Excision, and Infibulation: the Facts and Proposals for Change**, Report No. 47, London, 1983.
– **Latin American Women**, Report No. 57, London, 1983.
– **The Refugee Dilemma**, Report No. 43, London, 1981 (revised).
– **Western Europe's Migrant Workers**, Report No. 28, London, 1982.
– **Women in Asia**, Report No. 45, London, 1982.

Miss Universe, Inc., **Souvenir Program, 1985**, California.

Miss World, **Souvenir Programme, 1984** and **1985**, London.

MOEN, Elizabeth Williams, 'Genital mutilation: every woman's problem', **Working Paper No. 22**, Michigan, Michigan State University, 1983.

MOORE-CAVAR, Emily Campbell, **International Inventory of Information on Induced Abortion**, New York, Columbia University, International Institute for the Study of Human Reproduction, 1974.

MORGAN, Robin, ed., **Sisterhood is Global: The International Women's Movement Anthology**, Garden City, NY, Anchor Press, 1984.

MUKHOPADHYAY, M., **Silver Shackles**, Oxfam, 1984.

**Multinational Monitor**, 'By the sweat of her brow: women and multinationals', Vol. 4, No. 8, Aug 1983.

**N**

NASH, June and Helen Safa, **Women and Change in Latin America**, Bergin & Garvey Publishers, 1985.

National Commission on Working Women, **Women and the Vote – 1984; A Fact Sheet**, Washington DC, 1984.

National Women's Health Network, **Network News** (bi-monthly), Washington DC.

NATO Information Service, **Women in the NATO Forces**, 1984.

**New Internationalist** (monthly), London.

**New Internationalist**, **Women: A World Report**, London, Methuen, 1985.

New Internationlist, 'Where water is most unsafe', London, Oct 1984.

NEWLAND, Kathleen, 'Infant mortality and the health of societies', **Worldwatch Paper**, No. 47, Washington DC, Worldwatch Institute, 1981.
– **The Sisterhood of Man**, New York, W.W. Norton & Co., 1979.
– 'Women, men, and the division of labor', **Worldwatch Paper**, No. 37, Washington DC, Worldwatch Institute, 1980.

New York Times, 'Equality remains an elusive goal for United Nations women', 11 September 1985.

New York Times, 'Focus of UN food day tomorrow: women', 15 October 1984.

Newsweek, 'Rape and the law', 20 May 1985.

NORTMAN, Dorothy L., **Population and Family Planning Programs**, New York, Population Council, 1982, (11th edition).

# O

OECD, **The Role of Women in the Economy**, Paris, OECD, 1975.

**Off Our Backs** (monthly), Washington DC.

OGUNMODEDE, Esther, 'Genital mutilation', **ISIS International Bulletin**, No. 8, Geneva, n.d.

OHSE, Ulla, **Forced Prostitution and Traffic in Women in West Germany**, Edinburgh, Human Rights Group, 1984.

OWEN, Margaret, 'The traditional birth attendant and the law', **World Health Forum**, Vol. 4, No. 4, 1983.

# P

PAHO (Pan American Health Organization), **Health Conditions in the Americas 1977–1980**, Scientific Publication No. 427, Washington DC, PAHO, 1982.

Pakistan, Ministry of Information and Broadcasting, Women's Division, **A Study of Female Crime**, Islamabad, 1981.
– Women's Division, **Women in Pakistan**, Islamabad, n.d.

PAQUOT, Elisabeth, ed., **Terre Des Femmes: Panorama de la Situation des Femmes dans le Monde**, Montreal, Editions du Boreal Express, 1982.

PAXMAN, John M., **Law and Planned Parenthood**, London, IPPF, 1980.

PERVAIZ, Seema, **Analysis of Mass Media Appealing to Women**, Islamabad, Government of Pakistan, n.d.

PHIZACKLEA, Annie, **One Way Ticket: Migration and Female Labour**, London, Routledge & Kegan Paul, 1983.

PHONGPAICHIT, Pasuk, **From Peasant Girls to Bangkok Masseuses**, Geneva, ILO, 1982.

Population Council, **Population and Development Review**, Vol. 10, No. 3, 1984.

Population Crisis Committee, 'Improving the status of women', **Draper Fund Report**, No. 9, New York, Population Crisis Committee, 1980.
– 'Population growth and economic development', **Population**, Feb 1985.
– 'Abortion', **Population**, Sept 1982.
– 'World population growth and global security', **Population**, Sept 1983.

(PIP) Population Information Program, Johns Hopkins University, 'Age at first marriage and fertility', **Population Reports**, Vol. 7, No. 6, Nov 1979.
– 'Laws and policies affecting fertility', **Population Reports**, Series E, No. 7, Nov 1984.
– 'Legal trends and issues in voluntary sterilization', **Population Reports**, Series E, No. 6, 1981.
– 'Oral contraceptives', **Population Reports**, Series A, No. 5, 1982.
– 'Traditional midwives and family planning', **Population Reports**, Series J, No. 22, May 1980.
– 'The world fertility survey', **Population Reports**, Series M, No. 3, July 1979.

Population Institute, **International Dateline** (monthly), New York.

PRADHAN, Bina, **Work Patterns of Women in Food Production**, Rome, FAO, 1983.

PRB (Population Reference Bureau), 'Adolescent fertility: worldwide concerns', **Population Bulletin**, Vol. 40, No. 2, April 1985.
– 'Family planning and marriage, 1970–1980' (wallchart), Washington DC, PRB, 1981.
– 'Fertility and the status of women' (wallchart), Washington DC, PRB, 1981.
– **Poverty in America: Trends and New Patterns**, June 1985.
– 'The changing American family', **Bulletin**, Vol. 38, No. 4, Oct 1983.
– 'World's women data sheet' (wallchart), Washington DC, PRB, 1980.

Puget Sound Women's Peace Camp, **We Are Ordinary Women**, Seattle, Seal Press, 1985.

# Q

QUINN-JUDGE, Sophie, **Vietnamese Women: Neglected Promises**, Washington DC, Centre for International Policy, 1983.

# R

RAMPRAKASH, Deo, ed., **Social Trends**, London, HMG Stationery Office, 1986.

REDDY, A.K.N., et al., **Rural Energy Consumption Patterns – A Field Study**, Bangalore, ASTRA, Indian Institute of Science, 1980.

ROBERTSON, Patrick, **The Book of Firsts**, New York, Bramhall House, 1982.

ROBINS-MOWRY, D., **The Hidden Sun – Women in Modern Japan**, Colorado, Westview Press, 1983.

ROGERS, Barbara, **The Domestication of Women: Discrimination in Developing Societies**, London, Tavistock Publications, 1980.

ROGERS, Barbara, 'Women and land rights', **ISIS International Bulletin**, No. 11, Spring 1979.

ROSSI, A. and A. Calderwood, eds., **Academic Women on the Move**, New York, Russell Sage, 1973.

ROYSTON, E., 'The prevalence of nutritional anemia in women in developing countries: a critical review of available information', **World Health Statistics Quarterly**, No. 2, 1982.

RUSSELL, Diana E., **Rape in Marriage**, New York, Macmillan & Co., 1982.

RUSSELL, Diana and Nicole Van de Ven, **The Proceedings of the International Tribunal on Crimes Against Women**, East Palo Alto CA, Frog in the Well, 1984.

RYTINA, Nancy, 'Earnings of men and women', **Monthly Labor Review**, US Department of Labor, April 1982.

# S

SAFILIOS-ROTHSCHILD, Constantina, **Conventional and Nonconventional Socio-economic Indicators of Women's Status in the Third World**, New York, The Population Council, 1983.

SANCHEZ-TORRES, Fernando, 'Illegal abortion in Latin America', **Draper Fund Report**, No. 9, Oct 1980.

SALVAGE, Jane, **The Politics of Nursing**, London, Heinemann Medical Books, 1985.

SCHERER, John L., ed., **China Facts and Figures Annual**, Gulf Breeze Fla., Academic International Press, 1983 and 1984.

SCHIRMER, Jennifer, **The Limits of Reform: Women, Capital and Welfare**, Cambridge MA, Schenkman Publishing, 1982.

SCOTT, Hilda, **Working Your Way to the Bottom: The Feminization of Poverty**, Boston, Pandora Press, 1984.

SHAUL, Marnie, 'The status of women in local governments', **Public Administration Review**, Nov/Dec 1982.

SIVARD, Ruth Leger, **Women . . . A World Survey**, Washington DC, World Priorities, 1985.

Social and Cultural Planning Bureau, The Netherlands, **Women on the Move**, July 1985.

**Spare Rib** (monthly), London.

STALLARD, Karin, et al., **Poverty in the American Dream: Women and Children First**, Boston, South End Press, 1983.

State Statistical Bureau, People's Republic of China, **Statistical Yearbook of China**, 1983, 1984.

**Statistical Abstract of Latin America**, 1982.

**Statistical Yearbook for Asia and the Pacific**, 1982.

Statistics Sweden, **Women and Men in Sweden: Facts and Figures**, 1985.

STERN, Richard, 'The grease trade skids', **Forbes**, 25 October 1982.

# T

The 1985 IMS/Ayer Directory of Publications, Fort Washington Pa., IMS Press, 1985.
THITSA, Khin, 'Image and reality for women in Buddhist Thailand', **Change International Reports**, London, 1980.
TIETZE, Christopher, 'Maternal mortality excluding abortion mortality', **World Health Statistics Reports**, Vol. 30, No. 4, 1977.
– Induced Abortion. A World Review 1983, New York, Population Council, 1983 (fifth edition).

# U

Ulrich's International Periodicals Directory, New York, R.R. Bowker Co., 1985.

UN (United Nations), **Compendium of Social Statistics: 1977**, New York, UN, 1980.
– Demographic Yearbook (annual).
– Population and Vital Statistics Report: 1984. Special Supplement, New York, UN, 1984.
– Report of the World Conference of the International Women's Year (E/CONF.66/34), July 1975.
– World Population Trends and Policies: 1981 Monitoring Report and 1983 Monitoring Report, 1981 and 1983.

UN Commission on the Status of Women (annual reports).

UN Decade for Women (United Nations World Conference to Review and Appraise the Achievements of the United Nations Decade for Women: Equality, Development and Peace), **Development in Sectoral Areas. (A) Employment** (A/CONF.116/5/Add.2), Nairobi, Dec 1984.
– Development in Sectoral Areas. (B) Health and Nutrition (A/CONF.116/5/Add.3), Dec 1984.
– Development in Sectoral Areas. (C) Education (A/CONF.116/5/Add.4), Dec 1984.
– Development in Sectoral Areas. (H) Human Settlements (A/CONF.116/5/Add.90), 1985.
– Development in Sectoral Areas. (J) Refugee and Displaced Women (A/CONF.116/5/Add.11), Dec 1984.
– Development in Sectoral Areas. (K) Rural Development (A/CONF.116/5/Add.12), Dec 1984.
– Development in Sectoral Areas. (L) Science and Technology (A/CONF.116/5/Add.13), 1985.
– Report of the Secretary-General, Part One: General Trends in Equality, Development and Peace (A/CONF.116/5/Add.1), June 1985.
– Report of the World Conference to Review and Appraise the Achievements of the UN Decade for Women (A/CONF.116/28), July 1985.
– Review and Appraisal of the Progress Achieved and the Obstacles Encountered by the United Nations System at the Regional and International Levels (A/CONF.116/8), June 1985.
– Selected Statistics and Indicators on the Status of Women (A/CONF.116/10), May 1985.
– The State of the World's Women, 1985, 1985.
– World Survey on the Role of Women in Development (A/CONF.116/4) Dec 1984.

UN Division for Economic and Social Information, 'Strategies to improve the status of women over the next 15 years, 1985–2000', **Backgrounder**, No. 29, Sept 1985.

UNDP (United Nations Development Programme), 'Rural women's participation in development', **Evaluation Study, No. 3**, 1980.

UNECA (Economic Commission for Africa), **Day Care in Eastern Africa**, 1981.
– Demographic and Related Socio-Economic Data Sheets, 1983.
– Mozambique: Women, the Law, the Agrarian Reform, 1980.
– The Critical Needs of African Women and Appropriate Strategies in the Framework of the Gisenyi and Lusaka MULPOCs, 1981.

– Women of Africa Today and Tomorrow, 1975.

UN Economic and Social Council, **Inquiry on the Status of Combatting the Traffic in Persons**, (E/CN.4/sub2/AC.2/1982/13), 1982.
– Report on the Suppression of the Traffic in Persons and the Exploitation of the Prostitution of Others, 1983.

UNESCAP (UN Economic and Social Commission for Asia and the Pacific), 'Reflections on the decade for women', **Social Development Newsletter**, No. 10, April/July, 1984.
– Social Development Newsletter (quarterly).
– The Situation of Young Women in the Service and Entertainment Industries in the ESCAP Region (E/ESCAP/SD.3/17), 1982.

UNESCO (UN Educational, Scientific and Cultural Organization), **Statistical Yearbook** (annual).
– Tendances et projections des effectifs scolaires par degré d'enseignement et par age, 1960–2000. Paris, UNESCO, 1984.
– Women and Development: Indicators of Their Changing Role, Socio-economic Studies No. 3, Paris, 1981.

UN Expert Group on Fertility and Family, **Fertility and Family**, Proceedings of the International Conference on Population, New Delhi, Jan 1983.

UN Expert Group on Improving Statistics and Indicators on the Situation of Women, **Compiling Social Indicators on the Situation of Women. Technical Report** (ESA/STAT/AC.17/2), April 1983.

UN Fund for Population Activities, **Population Policy Compendium** (yearly).

UNHCR (UN High Commissioner for Refugees), 'A high rate of infant mortality', **Refugees**. No. 12, Dec 1984.
– Fact Sheets, various countries, 1985.
– Refugees (monthly).
– World Refugee Map, 1984.

UNICEF (UN Children's Emergency Fund), **Assignment Children** (quarterly).
– Situation Analysis of Children and Women in Kenya. Part Three: The Roles and Situation of Women, UNICEF and the Republic of Kenya, 1985.
– The State of the World's Children, 1984 and 1985, New York, Oxford University Press, 1983 and 1984.
– 'Women-headed households', **Assignment Children**, Spring 1980.

UNIESA (UN Department of International Economic and Social Affairs), **Directory of International Statistics, Volume I**, Statistical Series M, No. 56, 1982.
– Levels and Trends of Mortality since 1950, 1982.
– Marital Status and Fertility: A Comparable Analysis of WFS data for Twenty-One Countries, 1983.
– Marital Status and Fertility: Summary Report of an Analysis of World Fertility Survey Data, 1982.
– Selected Indicators on the Situation of Women, 1985 (wallchart), 1985.
– The World Population Situation in 1983, 1984.

UN International Drinking Water Supply and Sanitation Decade, **Decade Dossier**, New York, n.d.

UN Population Division, **Recent Levels and Trends in Contraceptive Use**, 1984.

UN World Assembly on Aging, **Introductory Document** (A/CONF.113/4), Mar 1982.

UN World Conference for Women (UN World Conference of the United Nations Decade for Women), **Descriptive List of National Machineries** (A/CONF.94/11/Add.1), July 1980.
– Report of the World Conference of the UN Decade for Women (A/CONF.94/35), July 1980.
– Review and Evaluation of Progress Achieved in the Implementation of the World Plan of Action: Education, 1980.
– Review and Evalation of Progress Achieved in the Implementation of the World Plan of Action: Health, 1980.
– Statistical Abstract (A/CONF.94/25), July 1980.
– Women in Rural Areas, 1980.

University of Colombo, **Status of Women: Sri Lanka**, Colombo, 1979.

URANG, Sally, 'The Pill and its marketing offspring', **Chemical Business**, July 25, 1983.

URDANG, Stephanie, 'The last transition? Women and development in Mozambique', **Review of African Political Economy**, Vol. 27/28, Feb 1984.

USAID (US Agency for International Development), Women in Development Office, **Women in International Migration**, June 1980.

US Commission on Civil Rights, **A Growing Crisis: Disadvantaged Women and Their Children**, 1983.

US Committee for Refugees, **World Refugee Survey**, 1983.

US Congress, Hearing before the Committee on Foreign Relations, US Senate, **Women in Development: Looking to the Future**, 7 June 1984.

US Congress, Office of Technology Assessment, **World Population and Fertility Planning Technologies: The Next Twenty Years**, Washington DC, 1982.

US Department of Commerce, Bureau of the Census, **Illustrative Statistics on Women in Selected Developing Countries**, Washington DC, US Department of Commerce, 1980.
– **Statistical Abstract of the United States, 1984**, Washington DC, US Government Printing Office, 1984 (104th edition).
– **Women of the World: A Chartbook for Developing Regions**, Washington DC, 1985.
– **Women of the World: Asia and the Pacific**, Nasra Shah (author), 1985.
– **Women of the World: Latin America and the Caribbean**, Elsa Chaney (author), 1984.
– **Women of the World: Near East and North Africa**, Mary Chamie (author), 1985.
– **Women of the World: Sub-Saharan Africa**, Jeanne S. Newman (author), 1984.

US Department of Justice, Bureau of Justice Statistics, **Report to the Nation on Crime and Justice: The Data**, Washington DC, US Department of Justice, Oct 1983.
– **The Crime of Rape**, Washington DC, US Department of Justice, 1985.

US Department of Labor, **Handbook of Labor Statistics**, 1983.
– **Time of Change: 1983 Handbook on Women Workers**, Bulletin No. 298, 1984.

US Department of State, **Country Background Reports**, various countries and years; continuous updating.

US National Center for Educational Statistics, **Digest of Education Statistics 1982**, Washington DC, US Government Printing Office, 1982.

**US News and World Report** (weekly).

# W

WAITE, Linda, 'US women at work', **Population Bulletin**, Vol. 36, No. 2, May 1981.

WAP (Women Against Pornography), promotional literature, 1985.

WARRIOR, Betsy, **Battered Women's Directory**, Cambridge MA, 1985 (9th edition).

**Washington Post**, 'Flesh supermarkets of the Third World', 3 March 1985.

WFS (World Fertility Survey), **World Fertility Survey: Major Findings and Implications**, 1984.

WFS and ISI (International Statistical Institute), 'Differentials in age at first marriage', **Comparative Studies: Cross-National Summaries**, No. 19, June 1982.

WHEELER, Hollis, 'Pornography and rape: a feminist perspective', in Burgess, **Rape and Sexual Assault**, *op. cit.*

WHO (World Health Organization ), **Bulletin of the World Health Organization**.
– **Coverage of Maternity Care**, Geneva, WHO, 1985.
– **Health and Status of Women**, Geneva, WHO, 1980.
– **Prevalence of Nutritional Anemia in Women in Developing Countries**, Geneva, WHO, 1979.
– **Sixth Report on the World Health Situation, 1980. Part One: Global Analysis**, Geneva, WHO, 1980.
– 'Women, development, and health', **World Health**, April 1985.
– **World Health Statistics**, (annual).
– **World Health Statistics Quarterly**.

WHO, EMRO (WHO, Regional Office for the Eastern Mediterranean), **Traditional Practices Affecting the Health of Women and Children**, Alexandria, WHO, 1982.

WILKIE, James W., ed., **Statistical Abstract of Latin America**, Vol. 20, Los Angeles, UCLA Latin America Centre Publications, 1980.

**WIN News** (quarterly), Lexington.

WISE, Peter, 'Portugal legalizes some abortions: vote threatens coalition', **Washington Post**, 28 January 1984.

WOLFSON, Alice, 'Access to abortion – the struggle continues', **Network News**, Nov/Dec 1983.

Women for Women Research and Study Group, **Situation of Women in Bangladesh**, Dacca, Women for Women/UNICEF, 1977.

Women in the Caribbean Project, **Women and the Family**, Vol. 2, 1982.

**Women of Europe** (bi-monthly), Commission of the European Communities, Brussels.

**Women Today**, 'Domestic violence and wife abuse', 22 March 1985.

**Women's Emergency Conference on the New Reproductive Technologies**, draft documentation, courtesy of Renate Duelli Klein, Lund, July 1985.

**Women's Peace Alliance**, international issue, June 1985.

World Bank, 'Health problems and policies in developing countries', **World Bank Staff Working Paper**, No. 412, 1980.
– 'Nutrition and food needs in developing countries', **World Bank Staff Working Paper**, No. 328, 1979.
– **Women in Development** (pamphlet), Washington DC, 1980.
– **World Development Report, 1976, 1984** and **1985**, New York, Oxford University Press, 1976, 1984, 1985.
– **World Tables: The Third Edition. Volume II: Social Data**, Baltimore, Johns Hopkins University Press, 1984.

World Pharmaceutical News, Scrip, 1981–1984.

# Y

YLLO, Kersti and Donald Finkelhor, 'Marital rape', in Burgess, **Rape and Sexual Assault**, *op. cit.*

# INDEX